# Praise for *The 5 Love Languages*

P9-EFJ-120

In our 39 years in the Army and especially in the years since 9/11/01, Paula and I have witnessed firsthand the extreme stress on many military marriages and the need for couples to build "emotional love resilience." As long-time practitioners of *The 5 Love Languages*, we are thrilled that military couples will now have a targeted version that speaks "their own language" and will help them renew their love for each other. You can have a successful military career and a healthy marriage—*The 5 Love Languages Military Edition* will help show you the way!

**~LTG (Ret.) R. L. VanAntwerp, U.S. Army**

A healthy military marriage is a tall order even in peacetime. Two wars and their aftermath have exacted an immeasurable toll on millions of service members and their spouses since 09-11-01. Chapman and Green's proven insights can help emotionally wounded military couples to speak the language of love even on the chaotic journey that is post-traumatic stress.

**~Marshele Carter Waddell, veteran Navy SEAL spouse and coauthor of *Wounded Warrior, Wounded Home: Hope and Healing for Families Living with PTSD and TBI***

When Barb and I learned that our two friends Jocelyn Green and Gary Chapman had teamed up to bring *The 5 Love Languages* to military marriages, we knew it was going to be a "1-2 punch"! And it is! The life message that Gary brings on the love languages through the experience and filter of Jocelyn Green, a star in the field of ministering to military families, offers the reader a powerful insight into strengthening their military home! Having ministered to military marriages ourselves, we know some of the unique needs of these heroic families. And we guarantee the reader this resource will further equip you to "crack the code" and learn how to better connect with your spouse! Read it and give it to every military family you know!

**~Dr. Gary and Barb Rosberg, America's Family Coaches, authors, *6 Secrets to a Lasting Love*, radio broadcasters, speakers, and passionate military marriage advocates**

For years, our family has communicated using *The 5 Love Languages* and found the results to be incredibly successful. Now, with the military version of this book, we are able to express love in an effective, encouraging, and empathetic manner that helps our military members and their families know how much we truly care about them. As the wife of a fighter pilot and mom to sons in the Marines, Air Force, and Army, I'm delighted to recommend this critical resource to the many military groups I address on a regular basis. Buy this book for your favorite military family as a way of thanking them for their service.

**~Ellie Kay, author of the bestselling *Heroes at Home*, "America's Military Family Expert"™**

I have used *The 5 Love Languages* over the past 12 years to conduct numerous marriage enrichment weekend events, in formal counseling with couples, informal counseling as I walk about ministering to people, and in dealing with leaders. The adaptation of the original *5 Love Languages* to a military focus will only enhance the positive effects this book produces. I firmly believe that this is not only one of the best books for relationship improvement, it is also one of the best leadership books on the market today. The ability to understand subordinate, peer, and senior love language needs improves every organization's relationships as leaders meet these needs. Thank you Dr. Chapman and Jocelyn Green for improving on a great book so that we might reach more effectively those Soldiers, Sailors, Airmen, Marines, and Coast Guardsmen to whom so many of our great ministers of faith have been called.

**~CH (MAJ) Scott Brown, U.S. Army**

As an Army wife of more than 25 years, I have lived the roller-coaster life of constant moves and separations. During my quest to find resources to help sustain a loving marriage I came across a lot of valuable research and advice, but it wasn't applicable for couples who face the stress of deployments and redeployments along with the fast tempo and demands of military life. FINALLY, Dr. Chapman's reputable work with *The 5 Love Languages* and Jocelyn Green's insight into military life have produced the perfect combination to help military couples see that a healthy, loving marriage and a successful military career are both possible. This is the book we have been seeking. What a treasured gift for our military families.

~**HOLLY SCHERER, military life consultant and coauthor of** *Military Spouse Journey;*
   *1001 Things to Love About Military Life;* **and** *Help! I'm A Military Spouse—I Get a Life*
   *Too!*

This is a must-have resource in a family's "kit bag." Dr. Chapman's work has enriched our lives on so many levels, and we are overjoyed there is a special edition that speaks directly to the military community. Effective communication is instrumental in building and sustaining resilience. Knowing how to speak your partner's love language is a wonderful tool to help maintain a strong, enduring, and joyful relationship.

~**NATE BROOKSHIRE, coauthor of** *Hidden Wounds: A Soldier's Burden*

*The 5 Love Languages Military Edition* provides a valuable tool for couples trying to build a strong relationship in the midst of the enormously challenging stresses of military service. It provides practical instruction on how to identify the true needs of your spouse and gives suggestions of actions to take that will be the most meaningful to them—all within the unique context of military cross-country moves, deployments, and reintegration. For those willing to make the sacrifices and put in the hard work, this book will be a useful guide to achieving a healthy, mature, and rewarding marriage.

~**RICHARD CROWLEY, Army spouse**

*The 5 Love Languages Military Edition* is exactly what every military marriage needs. The decoding section at the back of each chapter has great tips to keep the spark going while the military member is away, but these tips can also be used when the military member is at home. Once you and your spouse learn each other's love language, life becomes much sweeter.

~**MAUREEN ELIAS, Air Force spouse**

As military couples, we understand what is challenging about our marriages. Rarely do we find anyone willing to supply us with practical answers for those challenges—until Dr. Gary Chapman and Jocelyn Green in *The 5 Love Languages Military Edition*. This book will give you real help for the real struggles of military marriage.

~**CDR (RET.) ROBERT AND BETTINA DOWELL, U.S. Navy**

Teaching couples to discover their unique love language and learn to communicate their affection more strategically has been Dr. Chapman's mission for years. This military edition with Jocelyn Green considers the added challenges military families face, due to deployments and other geographical separations, making this book a must-have resource for chaplains, military support personnel, ministry leaders, and military couples alike. Buy more than one copy, because you will be sharing it with friends!

~**JILL BOZEMAN, Army spouse and founder of Operation Faithful Support**

# The 5 Love Languages

## MILITARY EDITION

### The Secret to Love That Lasts

# GARY CHAPMAN
## WITH JOCELYN GREEN

**NORTHFIELD PUBLISHING**

CHICAGO

All Scripture quotations are taken from the Holy Bible, New International Version®, NIV®. Copyright © 1973, 1978, 1984 by Biblica, Inc.™ Used by permission of Zondervan. All rights reserved worldwide www.zondervan.com. The "NIV" and "New International Version" are trademarks registered in the United States Patent and Trademark Office by Biblica, Inc.™

Edited by Elizabeth Cody Newenhuyse
Interior and cover design: Smartt Guys design
Cover image credits: Dog tags: Matt Smartt; Flag: Sergey Kamshylin / 123F
Authors photo credits: Gary Chapman-P.S. Photography / Jocelyn Green-Paul Kestel of
Catchlight Imaging

Chapman, Gary D.
    The 5 love languages military edition : the secret to love that lasts / Gary D Chapman, Jocelyn Green.
        pages cm
        Summary: "Marriage is hard enough for the everyday civilian. But imagine marriage when you're separated by thousands of miles . . . when one of you daily faces the dangers of combat . . . while the other shoulders all the burden of homefront duties. Add to that unpredictable schedules, frequent moves, and the challenge of reintegration, and it's no wonder military marriages are under stress. These men and women who are giving so much for so many need a way to love one another - a way that powerfully communicates to the heart. The 5 Love Languages has a successful track record of helping military couples heal broken relationships and strengthen healthy relationships. Now this #1 New York Times bestseller has been adapted specifically for military couples. Special features of the Military Edition include: Stories of military couples from every branch of service who have found ways to use the 5 love languages in their unique lifestyles. A Decoding Deployments section at the end of each love language chapter, offering tips on how to express love when you are apart. A new chapter, Love Language Scramblers, explains how to speak the love languages through some of the most challenging times of a military marriage. An updated Q&A section to include questions specific to military marriage. The 5 Love Languages profile will help you and your partner identify your love languages so you can put the principles to work for you immediately. Guided by input from dozens of military couples in all stages of their careers, authors Gary Chapman and former military wife Jocelyn Green offer you an unparalleled tool for your marriage with The 5 Love Languages Military Edition"-- Provided by publisher.
    Includes bibliographical references.
    ISBN 978-0-8024-0769-6 (pbk.)
    1. Military spouses--Psychology. 2. Military spouses--United States--Conduct of life. 3. Marriage. 4. Communication in marriage. 5. Self-help techniques. 6. Love. I. Green, Jocelyn. II. Title. III. Title: Five love languages military edition.
    UB403.C47 2013
    646.7'808835500973--dc23
                                                            2013022819

We hope you enjoy this book from Northfield Publishing. Our goal is to provide high-quality, thought-provoking books and products that connect truth to your real needs and challenges. For more information on other books and products that will help you with all your important relationships, go to 5lovelanguages.com or write to:

Northfield Publishing
820 N. La Salle Boulevard
Chicago, IL 60610


1 3 5 7 9 10 8 6 4 2

*Printed in the United States of America*

*To Karolyn,*
*Shelley, and Derek*

## Other Books by Gary Chapman

# Contents

# Acknowledgments

This military edition of *The 5 Love Languages* would not have been possible without the help of numerous contributors. First and foremost is Jocelyn Green. She knows the military lifestyle from personal experience. Her experience, her interviews with military couples, and her excellent writing skills have made this journey easy for me. I am deeply grateful to her.

Thanks also to my administrative assistant Anita Hall for her technical assistance, and to Betsey Newenhuyse at Northfield Publishing for her keen editorial skills.

For the past fifteen years, I have been speaking on military bases and listening to the stories of husbands and wives as they shared the stresses of daily military life. Many of them have given permission to use their stories in this edition. Of course, we have changed their names for the sake of privacy. I am sincerely grateful to each of these unnamed heroes, who have helped others by openly sharing their own experiences. Special thanks to Army wife Brenda Marlin for offering a host of ideas for our Decoding Deployments sections, to

Chaplain (Lt. Col.) Tom Cox for his valuable insights into the reintegration process, and to Paula and Lt. Gen. (Ret.) R. L. "Van" VanAntwerp for sharing wisdom gleaned from nearly four decades in the Army.

*The 5 Love Languages Military Edition* was informed by dozens of conversations, both recent and from years past, with members and spouses from all branches and ranks of the military. Thank you for your investment in military marriages through your contributions to this volume, and thank you for your service to our country.

# Introduction

I have been a marriage counselor for many years. I have never known of a couple who got married hoping to make each other miserable. Yet hundreds of couples have sat in my office sharing the deep pain of a fractured relationship.

Their dreams had turned to nightmares and they were ready to split. Through the process of counseling, I have seen many of those couples find renewed hope and learn the skills that create a loving, supportive marriage. One of the key elements in moving from failure to success is learning the power of love.

A number of years ago I wrote a book called *The 5 Love Languages*. It has sold more than eight million copies in English, and has been translated in more than forty languages around the world. Every week I receive emails saying, "Your book saved our marriage."

The book has been distributed widely to military couples, and the response has been extremely encouraging. One young man said, "As soon as I arrived in Afghanistan, I began reading *The 5 Love Languages*. I had never read anything so simple, yet so profound. This book enables marriages not only to survive through deployment but even thrive and deepen during the long period of separation."

I have led marriage enrichment seminars on numerous military bases, both in this country and abroad. Everywhere I go, those who seek to enrich military marriages have asked, "Why don't you write a Military Edition to *The 5 Love Languages* dealing with the unique challenges of military marriages?" This book is an attempt to answer that request.

Although exact statistics on divorce rates in the military are unavailable due to how such statistics are tracked, many chaplains have told me that numerous military marriages are under significant stress. Many couples are truly suffering. The adjustments of early marriage are often thwarted by an untimely deployment. What happens in the heart, mind, and behavior of the husband and wife during deployment often creates emotional distance. Reentry after deployment can often be traumatic. I believe the most essential ingredient in a successful military marriage is to keep emotional love alive in the relationship. What you are about to read has the potential of helping you have the marriage you've always wanted.

Author and former military wife Jocelyn Green has helped guide the shape of this edition and collected many stories you will read here about military marriages. The names have been changed to protect the privacy of the individuals. The branch of service and military rank of the individuals are usually unstated. The message of *The 5 Love Languages* applies to all military couples. If this book helps you, I hope you will share it with other military couples. I believe together we can help thousands of couples discover that a healthy marriage and a successful military career are both possible.

—GARY CHAPMAN

# THE 5 LOVE LANGUAGES®

# CHAPTER 1

# What Happens *to* Love *in a* Military Marriage?

I first met Chuck in Germany. He had a successful military career—twenty-three years under his belt. However, in his own words, "My marriage is in shambles. I don't understand love and I'm not sure you can keep love alive in a military marriage. I was madly in love with my first wife. We were high school sweethearts. We got married right after graduation, and a month later I joined the military. The first couple of years were exciting, but eventually our love grew cold. We seemed like roommates living in the same house. On the day after our tenth anniversary, she went home to visit her mother and never returned. I didn't feel all that bad about it because by this time neither one of us loved each other."

"What about your second marriage?" I inquired.

"It was about a year after our divorce that I met Cathy. At the time, she was also in the military. It was one of those 'love at first sight deals,'" he said. "It was great. We had an awesome marriage until we got assigned to different bases. That was tough. So a year later, she left the military so we could be together. Then, the baby came along and things changed. We never rediscovered the connection we had in the first year of our marriage. It was like our love evaporated. She and our son left last Tuesday to go back to the States, and I know it's just a matter of time until she files for divorce."

"When things were going well, how did you express your love to Cathy?" I asked.

"I told her how beautiful she was. I told her I loved her. I told her how proud I was to be her husband. But after three or four years, she started complaining about petty things at first—like my not taking the garbage out, or my not hanging up my clothes. Later she went to attacking my character, telling me she didn't feel she could trust me, accusing me of being unfaithful to her. She became a totally negative person. When I met her she was one of the most positive people I had ever known. That's one of the things that attracted me to her; she never complained about anything. Everything I did was wonderful, but after a few years, I could do nothing right. I really think I tried. I honestly don't know what happened."

I could tell Chuck was experiencing internal struggle over what was going on in his marriage, so I said, "You still love Cathy, don't you?"

"I think I do," he said. "I don't have the kind of love I had when we first got married, but I certainly don't want a divorce. I think we could have made it, but I don't think Cathy wants to work on the marriage." I could tell this strong warrior had a wounded heart.

"Did things go downhill after the baby was born?" I asked.

"Yes," he said. "I felt like she gave all of her attention to the baby, and I no longer mattered. It was as if her goal in life was to have a baby, and after the baby she no longer needed me."

"Did you tell her that?" I asked.

"Yes, I told her. She said I was crazy. She said I did not understand the stress of being a twenty-four-hour nurse, and I should be more understanding and help her more. I really tried, but it didn't seem to make any difference. After that we just grew apart. After a while there was no love left, just deadness."

Chuck continued the conversation and I listened. "What happened to love after the first year of marriage?" he asked. "Is my experience common? Is that why we have so many divorces in the military? I can't believe this has happened to me twice. And those who don't divorce, do they learn to live with the emptiness, or does love really stay alive in some marriages?"

The questions Chuck asked are the questions thousands of military couples are asking. Sometimes the answers are couched in psychological research jargon that is almost incomprehensible. Sometimes they are couched in humor and folklore. Most of the jokes and pithy sayings contain some truth, but they are often like offering an aspirin to a person with cancer.

The desire for romantic love in marriage is deeply rooted in our psychological makeup. Books abound on the subject. Television and radio talk shows deal with it. The Internet is full of advice. So are our parents and friends. Keeping love alive in our marriages is serious business.

With all the help available from media experts, why is it so few couples seem to have found the secret to keeping love alive after the wedding?

## THE TRUTH WE'RE MISSING

The answer to those questions is the purpose of this book. It's not that the books and articles already published are not helpful. The problem is we have overlooked one fundamental truth: People speak different love languages.

★ ★ ★

*Your emotional love language and the language of your spouse may be as different as Chinese from English.*

My academic training is in the area of anthropology. Therefore, I have studied in the area of linguistics, which identifies a number of major language groups: Japanese, Chinese, Spanish, English, Portuguese, Greek, German, French, and so on. Most of us grow up learning the language of our parents and siblings, which becomes our *primary* or native tongue. Later, we may learn additional languages—but usually with much more effort. These become our *secondary* languages. We speak and understand best our native language. We feel most comfortable speaking that language. The more we use a secondary language, the more comfortable we become conversing in it. If we speak only our primary language and encounter someone else who speaks only his or her primary language, which is different from ours, our communication will be limited. We must rely on pointing, grunting, drawing pictures, or acting out our ideas. We can communicate, but it's awkward. Language differences are part and parcel of human culture. If we are to communicate effectively across cultural lines, we must learn the language of those with whom we wish to communicate.

In the area of love, it is similar. Your emotional love language and the language of your spouse may be as different as Chinese from English. No matter how hard you try to express love in English, if your spouse understands only Chinese, you will never understand how to love each other. Chuck was speaking the language of words of affirmation to Cathy when he told her she was beautiful, he loved her, and he was proud to be her husband. He was speaking love, and he was sincere, but she did not understand his language. Perhaps she was looking for love in his behavior and didn't see it. Being sincere is not enough. We must be willing to learn our spouse's primary love language if we are to effectively communicate love.

My conclusion after thirty-five years of marriage counseling is that there are five emotional love languages—five ways people speak and understand emotional love. In the field of linguistics a language may have numerous dialects or variations. Similarly, within the five basic emotional love languages, there are many dialects. That accounts for the magazine articles titled "10 Ways to Let Your Spouse Know You Love Her," "20 Ways to Keep Your Man at Home," or "365 Expressions of Marital Love." There are not 10, 20, or 365 basic love languages. In my opinion, there are only five. However, there may be numerous dialects. The number of ways to express love within a love language is limited only by one's imagination. The important thing is to speak the love language of your spouse.

Seldom do a husband and wife have the same primary emotional love language. We tend to speak our primary love language, and we become confused when our spouse does not understand what we are communicating. We are expressing our love, but the message does not come through because we are speaking what, to them, is a foreign language. Therein lies the fundamental problem, and it is the purpose of this book to offer a solution. That's why I dare to write another book on love. Once we discover the five basic love languages and understand our own primary love language, as well as the primary love language of our spouse, we will then have the needed information to apply the ideas in the books and articles.

Once you identify and learn to speak your spouse's primary love language, I believe you will have discovered the key to a long-lasting, loving marriage. These languages can be spoken even when you are separated by deployment. Love need not evaporate after the wedding, but in order to keep it alive most of us will have to put forth the effort to learn a secondary love language. We cannot rely on our native tongue if our spouse does not understand it. If we want them to feel the love we are trying to communicate, we must express it in his or her primary love language.

**YOUR TURN**

*Complete the following: "There would be fewer divorces if only people*
_____.*"*

# THE 5 LOVE LANGUAGES®

# CHAPTER 2

# Keeping *the* Love Tank Full

Love is the most important word in the English language—and the most confusing. Both secular and religious thinkers agree that love plays a central role in life. Thousands of books, songs, magazines, and movies are peppered with the word. Numerous philosophical and theological systems have made a prominent place for love.

Psychologists have concluded that the need to feel loved is a primary human emotional need. For love, we will climb mountains, cross seas, traverse desert sands, and endure untold hardships. Without love, mountains become unclimbable, seas uncrossable, deserts unbearable, and hardships our lot in life.

If we can agree that the word *love* permeates human society, both historically and in the present, we must also agree it's a most confusing word. We use it in a thousand ways. We say, "I love hot dogs," and in the next breath, "I love my mother." We speak of loving activities: swimming, skiing, hunting. We love objects: food, cars, houses. We love animals: dogs, cats, even pet snails. We love nature: trees, grass, flowers, and weather. We love people: mother, father, son, daughter, wives, husbands, friends. We even fall in love with love.

If all that is not confusing enough, we also use the word *love* to explain behavior. "I did it because I love her." That explanation is given for all kinds of actions. A politician is involved in an adulterous relationship, and he calls it love. However, most of his constituents call it stupidity. The preacher, on the other hand, calls it sin. The wife of an alcoholic picks up the pieces after her husband's latest episode. She calls it love, but the psychologist calls it codependency. The parent indulges all the child's wishes, calling it love. The family therapist would call it irresponsible parenting. What is loving behavior?

The purpose of this book is not to eliminate all confusion surrounding the word *love*, but to focus on that kind of love that is essential to our emotional health. Child psychologists affirm that every child has certain basic emotional needs that must be met if he is to be emotionally stable. Among those emotional needs, none is more basic than the need for love and affection, the need to sense that he or she belongs and is wanted. With an adequate supply of affection, the child will likely develop into a responsible adult. Without that love, he or she will be emotionally and socially challenged.

I liked the metaphor the first time I heard it: "Inside every child is an 'emotional tank' waiting to be filled with love. When a child really feels loved, he will develop normally but when the love tank is empty, the child will misbehave. Much of the misbehavior of children is motivated by the cravings of an empty 'love tank.'" I was listening to Dr. Ross Campbell, a psychiatrist who specialized in the treatment of children and adolescents.

As I listened, I thought of the hundreds of parents who had paraded the misdeeds of their children through my office. I had never visualized an empty love tank inside those children, but I had certainly seen the results of it. Their misbehavior was a misguided search for the love they did not feel. They were seeking love in all the wrong places and in all the wrong ways.

I remember Ashley, who at thirteen years of age was being treated for a sexually transmitted disease. Her military parents were crushed. They were angry with Ashley. They were upset with the school, which they blamed for teaching her about sex. "Why would she do this?" they asked.

In my conversation with Ashley, she told me of her parents' divorce when she was six years old. "I thought my father left because he didn't love me," she said. "When my mother remarried when I was ten, I felt she now had someone to love her, but I still had no one to love me. I wanted so much to be loved. I met this boy at school. He was older than me, but he liked me. I couldn't believe it. He was kind to me, and in a while I really felt he loved me. I didn't want to have sex, but I wanted to be loved."

★ ★ ★

We needed love before we "fell in love," and we will need it as long as we live.

Ashley's "love tank" had been empty for many years. Her mother and stepfather had provided for her physical needs but had not realized the deep emotional struggle raging inside her. They certainly loved Ashley, and they thought she felt their love. Not until it was almost too late did they discover they were not speaking Ashley's primary love language.

The emotional need for love, however, is not simply a childhood phenomenon. That need follows us into adulthood and into marriage. The "in love" experience temporarily meets that need, but has a limited and predictable life span. After we come down from the high of the "in love" obsession, the emotional need for love resurfaces because it is fundamental to our nature. It's at the center of our emotional desires. We needed love before we "fell in love," and we will need it as long as we live.

The need to feel loved by one's spouse is at the heart of marital desires. A man said to me recently, "What good is the house, the cars, the place at the beach, or any of the rest of it if your wife doesn't love you?" Do you understand what he was really saying? "More than anything, I want to be loved by my wife." Material things are no replacement for human, emotional love. A wife says, "He ignores me all day long and then wants to jump in bed with me. I hate it." She is not a wife who hates sex; she is a wife desperately pleading for emotional love.

## OUR CRY FOR LOVE

Something in our nature cries out to be loved by another. Isolation is devastating to the human psyche. That's why solitary confinement is considered the cruelest of punishments. At the heart of humankind's existence is the desire to be intimate and to be loved by another. Marriage is designed to meet that need for intimacy and love. If the need for love is not met, the intimacy we thought we had evaporates and the marriage seems empty. But if love is important, it's also elusive. I have listened to many military couples share their secret pain. Some came to me because the inner ache had become unbearable. Others came because they realized their behavior patterns or the misbehavior of their spouse was destroying the marriage. Some came simply to inform me they no longer wanted to be married. Their dreams of "living happily ever after" had been dashed against the hard walls of reality. Again and again I have heard the words "Our love is gone; our relationship is dead. We used to feel close, but not now. We no longer enjoy being with each other. We don't meet each other's needs." Their stories bear testimony that adults as well as children have "love tanks."

Could it be that deep inside hurting couples exists an invisible "emotional love tank" with its gauge on empty? Could the misbehavior, withdrawal, harsh words, and critical spirit occur because of that empty tank? If we could find a way to fill it, could the marriage be reborn? With a full tank would couples be able to create an emotional climate where it's possible to discuss differences and resolve conflicts? Could that tank be the key that makes marriage work?

Those questions sent me on a long journey. Along the way, I discovered the simple yet powerful insights contained in this book. The journey has taken me not only through thirty-five years of marriage counseling but into the hearts and minds of hundreds of military couples throughout America. From Seattle to Miami, couples have invited me into the inner chamber of their marriages, and we have talked openly. The illustrations included in this book are cut from the fabric of real life. Only names and places are changed to protect the privacy of the individuals who have spoken so freely.

Keeping the emotional love tank full is as important to a marriage as maintaining the proper oil level is to an automobile. Running your marriage on an empty "love tank" may cost you even more than trying to drive your car without oil. What you are about to read has the potential of saving thousands of marriages and can even enhance the emotional climate of a good marriage. Whatever the quality of your marriage now, it can always be better.

**WARNING:** Understanding the five love languages and learning to speak the primary love language of your spouse may radically affect his or her behavior. People behave differently when their emotional love tanks are full.

Before we examine the five love languages, however, we must address one other important but confusing phenomenon: the euphoric experience of "falling in love."

## YOUR TURN

1. *On a scale of 0 to 10, how full is your love tank? Why do you think this is true?*

2. *Would you be willing to ask your spouse for a love tank report?*
   - *You might ask, "On a scale of 0 to 10, how full is your love tank?"*
   - *If their answer is anything less than 10, you might say, "What could I do to help fill it?"*
   - *Let their answer guide you to a meaningful expression of love.*

# THE 5 LOVE LANGUAGES®

# CHAPTER 3

# Falling *in* Love

She showed up at my office without an appointment and asked my secretary if she could see me for five minutes. I had known Janice for eighteen years. She was thirty-six and had never married. From time to time, she had made appointments with me to discuss a particular difficulty in one of her dating relationships. She was by nature a conscientious caring person, so it was completely out of character for her to show up at my office unannounced. I thought, *There must be some terrible crisis for Janice to come without an appointment.* I told my assistant to show her in, and I fully expected to see her burst into tears and tell me some tragic story as soon as the door was closed. Instead, she practically skipped into my office, beaming with excitement.

"How are you today, Janice?" I asked.

"Great!" she said. "I've never been better in my life. I'm getting married!"

"You *are*?" I said. "To whom and when?"

"To David Gallespie," she exclaimed. "He's in the military, and I've always wanted to travel."

"That's exciting. How long have you been dating?"

"Three weeks. I know it's crazy, Dr. Chapman, after all the people I have dated and the number of times I came so close to getting married. I can't believe it myself, but I know David is the one for me. From the first date, we both knew it. Of course, we didn't talk about it on the first night, but one week later, he asked me to marry him. I knew he was going to ask me, and I knew I was going to say yes. I have never felt this way before. You know about the relationships I have had through the years and the struggles I have had. In every relationship, something was not right. I never felt at peace about marrying any of them, but I know David is the right one."

By this time, Janice was rocking back and forth in her chair, giggling and saying, "I know it's crazy, but I am so happy. I've never been this happy in my life."

What has happened to Janice? She has fallen in love. In her mind, David is the most wonderful man she has ever met. He is perfect in every way. He will make the ideal husband. She thinks about him day and night. The fact that David has been married twice before, has three children, and has been in the military for fifteen years are trivial to Janice. She's happy, and she is convinced she is going to be happy forever with David. She is in love.

Most of us enter marriage by way of the "in love" experience. We meet someone whose physical characteristics and personality traits create enough electrical shock to trigger our "love alert" system. The bells go off, and we set in motion the process of getting to know the person. The first step may be sharing a hamburger or steak, depending on our budget, but our real interest is not in the food. We are on a quest to discover love. "Could this warm, tingly feeling I have inside be the 'real' thing?"

Sometimes we lose the tingles on the first date. We find out he spends time on crackpot websites or she attended six colleges, and the tingles run right out our toes; we want no more hamburgers with them. Other times, however, the tingles are stronger after the hamburger than before. We arrange for a few more "together" experiences, and before long the level of intensity has increased to the point where we find ourselves saying, "I'm falling in love." Eventually we are convinced it's the "real thing," and we tell the other person, hoping the feeling is reciprocal. If it isn't, things cool off a bit or we redouble our efforts to impress, and eventually win the love of, our beloved. When it's reciprocal, we start talking about marriage because everyone agrees being "in love" is the necessary foundation for a good marriage.

## THE ANTEROOM OF HEAVEN

At its peak, the "in love" experience is euphoric. We are emotionally obsessed with each other. We go to sleep thinking of one another. When we rise, that person is the first thought on our minds. We long to be together. Spending time together is like playing in the anteroom of heaven. When we hold hands, it seems as if our blood flows together. We could kiss forever if we didn't have to go to school or work. Embracing sparks dreams of marriage and ecstasy.

The person who is "in love"—we'll call her Jen—has the illusion that her beloved is perfect. Her best friend can see the flaws—it bothers her how he talks to Jen sometimes—but Jen won't listen. Her mother, noting the young man seems unable to hold a steady job, keeps her concerns to herself but asks polite questions about "Ryan's plans."

Our dreams before marriage are of marital bliss: "We are going to make each other supremely happy. Other couples may argue and fight, but not us. We love each other." Of course, we are not totally naive. We know intellectually we will eventually have differences. But we are certain we will discuss those differences openly; one of us will always be willing to make concessions, and we will reach agreement. It's hard to believe anything else when you are in love.

We have been led to believe if we are really in love, it will last forever. We will always have the wonderful feelings we have at this moment. Nothing could ever come between us. Nothing will ever overcome our love for each other. We are caught up in the beauty and charm of the other's personality. Our love is the most wonderful thing we have ever experienced. We observe some married couples seem to have lost that feeling, but it will never happen to us. "Maybe they didn't have the real thing," we reason.

Unfortunately, the eternality of the "in love" experience is fiction, not fact. The late psychologist Dr. Dorothy Tennov conducted long-range studies on the "in love" phenomenon. After studying scores of couples, she concluded the average life span of a romantic obsession is two years. If it's a secretive love affair, it may last a little longer. Eventually, however, we all descend from the clouds and plant our feet on earth again. Our eyes are opened, and we see the warts of the other person. Her "quirks" are now genuinely annoying. He shows a capacity for hurt and anger, perhaps even harsh words and critical judgments. Those little traits we overlooked when we were in love now become huge mountains.

## REALITY INTRUDES

Welcome to the real world of marriage, where hairs are always on the sink and little white spots cover the mirror, where arguments center on which way the toilet paper comes off and whether the lid should be up or down. It's a world where shoes do not walk to the closet and drawers do not close themselves, where coats do not like hangers and socks go AWOL during laundry. In this world, a look can hurt and a word can crush. Intimate lovers can become enemies, and marriage a battlefield.

What happened to the "in love" experience? Alas, it was but an illusion by which we were tricked into signing our names on the dotted line, for better or for worse. No wonder so many have come to curse marriage and the partner whom they once loved. After all, if we were deceived, we have a right to be angry. Did we really have the "real" thing? I think so. The problem was faulty information.

The bad information was the idea that the "in love" obsession would last forever. We should have known better. A casual observation should have taught us that if people remained obsessed, we would all be in serious trouble. The shock waves would rumble through business, industry, military, education, and the rest of society. Why? Because people who are "in love" lose interest in other pursuits. That is why we call it an "obsession." The college student who falls head over heels in love sees his grades tumbling. It's difficult to study when you are in love. Tomorrow you have a test on the War of 1812, but who cares about the War of 1812? When you're in love, everything else seems irrelevant. A man said to me, "Dr. Chapman, my job is disintegrating."

"What do you mean?" I asked.

"I met this girl, fell in love, and I can't get a thing done. I can't keep my mind on my job. I spend my day dreaming about her."

The euphoria of the "in love" state gives us the illusion we have an intimate relationship. We feel we belong to each other. We believe we can conquer all problems. We feel altruistic toward each other. As one young man said about his fiancée, "I can't conceive of doing anything to hurt her. My only desire is to make her happy. I would do anything to make her happy." Such obsession gives us the false sense that our egocentric attitudes have been eradicated and we have become sort of a Mother Teresa, willing to give anything for the benefit of our lover. The reason we can do that so freely is that we sincerely believe that our lover feels the same way toward us. We believe she is committed to meeting our needs; he loves us as much as we love him and would never do anything to hurt us.

That thinking is always fanciful. Not that we are insincere in what we think and feel, but we are unrealistic. We fail to reckon with the reality of human nature. By nature, we are egocentric. Our world revolves around us. None of us is totally altruistic. The euphoria of the "in love" experience only gives us that illusion.

Once the experience of falling in love has run its natural course (remember, the average "in love" experience lasts two years), we will return to the world of reality and begin to assert ourselves. He will express his desires, but his desires will be different from hers. He wants sex, but she is too tired. He dreams of buying a new car, but she flatly says, "We can't afford it." She would like to visit her parents, but he says, "I don't like spending so much time with your family." Little by little, the illusion of intimacy evaporates, and the individual desires, emotions, thoughts, and behavior patterns assert themselves. They are two individuals. Their minds have not melded together, and their emotions mingled only briefly in the ocean of love. Now the waves of reality begin to separate them. They fall out of love, and at that point either they withdraw, separate, divorce, and set off in search of a new "in love" experience, or they begin the hard work of learning to love each other without the euphoria of the "in love" obsession.

Some military couples believe the end of the "in love" experience means they have only two options: resign themselves to a life of misery with their spouse, or jump ship and try again. Our generation has opted for the latter, whereas an earlier generation often chose the former. Before we automatically conclude we have made the better choice, perhaps we should examine the data. Currently 40 percent of first marriages in this country end in divorce. Sixty percent of second marriages and 73 percent of third marriages end the same way.[1] Apparently the prospect of a happier marriage the second and third time around is not substantial.

Research seems to indicate there is a third and better alternative: We can recognize the "in love" experience for what it was—a temporary emotional high—and now pursue "real love" with our spouse. That kind of love is emotional in nature but not obsessional. It's a love that unites reason and emotion. It involves an act of the will and requires discipline, and it recognizes the need for personal growth. Our most basic emotional need is not to fall in love but to be genuinely loved by another, to know a love that grows out of reason and choice, not instinct. I need to be loved by someone who chooses to love me, who sees in me something worth loving.

That kind of love requires effort and discipline. It is the choice to expend energy in an effort to benefit the other person, knowing that if his or her life is enriched by your effort, you too will find a sense of satisfaction—the satisfaction of having genuinely loved another. It does not require the euphoria of the "in love" experience. In fact, true love cannot begin until the "in love" experience has run its course.

We cannot take credit for the kind and generous things we do while under the influence of "the obsession." We are pushed and carried along by an instinctual force that goes beyond our normal behavior patterns. But if, once we return to the real world of human choice, we choose to be kind and generous, that is real love.

The emotional need for love must be met if we are to have emotional health. Married adults long to feel affection and love from their spouses. We feel secure when we are assured our mate accepts us, wants us, and is committed to our well-being. During the "in love" stage, we felt all of those emotions. It was heavenly while it lasted. Our mistake was in thinking it would last forever.

But that obsession was not meant to last forever. In the textbook of marriage, it is but the introduction. The heart of the book is rational, volitional love. That is the kind of love to which the sages have always called us. It's intentional.

That is good news to the military couple who have lost all of their "in love" feelings. If love is a choice, then they have the capacity to love after the "in love" obsession has died and they have returned to the real world. That kind of love begins with an attitude—a way of thinking. Love is the attitude that says, "I am married to you, and I choose to look out for your interests." Then the one who chooses to love will find appropriate ways to express that decision.

"But it seems so sterile," some may contend. "Love as an attitude with appropriate behavior? Where are the shooting stars, the balloons, the deep emotions? What about the spirit of anticipation, the twinkle of the eye, the electricity of a kiss, the excitement of sex? What about the emotional security of knowing I am number one in their mind?" That is what this book is all about. How do we meet each other's deep, emotional need to feel loved? If we can learn that and choose to do it, then the love we share will be exciting beyond anything we ever felt when we were infatuated.

For many years now, I have discussed the five emotional love languages in my marriage seminars and in private counseling sessions. Thousands of military couples will attest to the validity of what you are about to read. My files are filled with letters from people whom I have never met, saying, "A friend loaned me your book on love languages, and it has revolutionized our marriage. We had struggled for years trying to love each other, but our efforts had missed each other emotionally. Now that we are speaking the appropriate love languages, the emotional climate of our marriage has radically improved."

When your spouse's emotional love tank is full and he feels secure in your love, the whole world looks bright and your spouse will move out to reach his highest potential in life. But when the love tank is empty and he feels used but not loved, the whole world looks dark and he will likely never reach his potential for good in the world. In the next five chapters, I will explain the five emotional love languages and then, in chapter 10, illustrate how discovering your spouse's primary love language can make your efforts at love most productive.

## YOUR TURN

*Look back on that point in your marriage when "reality" set in and the initial romantic feelings faded. How did this affect your relationship, for better or worse?*

# THE 5 LOVE LANGUAGES®

# CHAPTER 4

LOVE LANGUAGE #1

# Words *of* Affirmation

ark Twain once said, "I can live for two months on a good compliment." If we take Twain literally, six compliments a year would have kept his emotional love tank at the operational level. Your spouse will probably need more.

One way to express love emotionally is to use words that build up. Solomon, author of the ancient Hebrew wisdom literature, wrote, "The tongue has the power of life and death."[2] Many couples have never learned the tremendous power of verbally affirming each other. Solomon further noted, "An anxious heart weighs a man down, but a kind word cheers him up."[3]

Verbal compliments, or words of appreciation, are powerful communicators of love. They are best expressed in simple, straightforward statements of affirmation, such as:

"You look sharp in that suit."

THE 5 LOVE LANGUAGES • MILITARY EDITION

"Do you ever look hot in that dress! Wow!"

"I really like how you're always on time to pick me up at work."

"Thanks for getting the babysitter lined up tonight. I don't take that for granted."

"I love how you are so responsible. I feel like I can count on you."

What would happen to the emotional climate of a marriage if the husband and wife heard such words of affirmation regularly?

Several years ago, I was sitting in my office with my door open. A lady walking down the hall said, "Have you got a minute?"

"Sure, come in."

She sat down and said, "Dr. Chapman, I've got a problem. I can't get my husband to paint our bedroom. I have been after him for nine months. I have tried everything I know, and I can't get him to paint it."

I said, "Tell me about it."

She said, "Well, last Saturday was a good example. You remember how pretty it was? Do you know what my husband did all day long? He worked on updating his computer!"

"So what did you do?"

"I went in there and said, 'Dan, I don't understand you. Today would have been a perfect day to paint the bedroom, and here you are working on your computer.'"

"So did he paint the bedroom?" I inquired.

"No. It's still not painted. I don't know what to do."

"Let me ask you a question," I said. "Are you opposed to computers?"

"No, but I want the bedroom painted."

"Are you certain your husband knows that you want the bedroom painted?"

"I know he does," she said. "I've been after him for nine months."

"Let me ask you one more question. Does your husband ever do anything good?"

"Like what?"

"Oh, like taking the garbage out, or getting bugs off the windshield of the car you drive, or putting gas in the car, or hanging up his coat?"

"Yes," she said, "he does some of those things."

"Then I have two suggestions. One, don't ever mention painting the bedroom again." I repeated, "Don't ever mention it again."

"I don't see how that's going to help," she said.

"Look, you just told me he knows you want the bedroom painted. You don't have to tell him anymore. He already knows. The second suggestion I have is that the next time your husband does anything good, give him a verbal compliment. For example, if he takes the garbage out, say, 'Dan, I want you to know I really appreciate your taking the garbage out.' Don't say, 'About time you took the garbage out. The flies were going to carry it out for you.' Every time he does anything good, give him a verbal compliment."

"I don't see how that's going to get the bedroom painted."

I said, "You asked for my advice. You have it. It's free."

She wasn't very happy with me when she left. Three weeks later, however, she came back to my office and said, "It worked!" She had learned that verbal compliments are far greater motivators than nagging words.

I'm not suggesting verbal flattery

— ★★★ —

The latent potential within your spouse in his or her areas of insecurity may await your encouraging words.

in order to get your spouse to do something you want. The object of love is not getting something you want but doing something for the well-being of the one you love. It's a fact, however, that when we receive affirming words we are far more likely to be motivated to reciprocate and do something our spouse desires.

## ENCOURAGING WORDS

Giving verbal compliments is only one way to express words of affirmation to your spouse. Another dialect is encouraging words. The word *encourage* means "to inspire courage." All of us have areas in which we feel insecure. We lack courage, and lack of courage often hinders us from accomplishing the positive things we would like to do. The latent potential within your spouse in his or her areas of insecurity may await your encouraging words.

Though Tricia had once been active duty herself, after she transitioned out, her identity became wrapped up in her roles as wife and mother. When an ombudsman position opened at Goodfellow Air Force Base in San Angelo, Texas, her husband, Greg, encouraged her to take it. The ombudsman is the spouse liaison for the command, answers directly to the commanding officer of a command, and is the person dependent spouses are supposed to be able to call whenever they have a question about their spouse's job.

"You can do this," Greg told Tricia. "Since you were active duty Navy yourself, you would be able to bring an interesting perspective."

Bolstered by her husband's words, Tricia volunteered. But when she learned her training would require a trip away from her family, she balked. "That trip was the first I would ever make ALONE to do something just for myself, aside from the occasional day out shopping," she remembered. "It was a week long, was taking place over Valentine's Day, and I had no idea what I would do without my children as my security blanket. Greg practically had to force me to drive away. Until I was about halfway to my destination, I kept wanting to turn around and go home. However, it turned out to be a fantastic trip. In addition to my training, I got to go to the beach and spend time alone, which was very relaxing. "

Greg encouraged Tricia to enjoy her own interests, even though it sometimes meant sending her away. Tricia said, "Ever since my first duty station (as a student fresh out of boot camp) in Monterey, California, I've been in love with the beach. My husband knew this. When we were stationed in Augusta, Georgia, however, our kids were young and we didn't know people we could ask to babysit them so we could have a weekend away. So Greg suggested I go to Myrtle Beach while he stayed home with the kids."

At first, Tricia felt like he was just trying to have time away from her. But she went, and came back feeling recharged, refreshed, and more in touch with herself. "Those trips gave me time to realize what was important to me, and to realize my husband was concerned for my well-being. Greg loved me enough to help me explore things I loved so that, in the event he did not return from one of his deployments, he could be confident I would not turn into a puddle of goo on the floor, a heaping, crying mess, unable to take care of myself, let alone my children."

Greg's encouraging words gave Tricia the strength she needed to develop her own potential.

Perhaps your spouse has untapped potential in one or more areas of life. That potential may be awaiting your encouraging words. Perhaps she needs to enroll in a course to develop that potential. Maybe he needs to meet some people who have succeeded in that area, who can give him insight on the next step he needs to take. Your words may give your spouse the courage necessary to take that first step.

Please note that I am not talking about pressuring your spouse to do something *you* want. I am talking about encouraging him to develop an interest he already has. For example, a wife might pressure her husband to look for a more lucrative job. The wife thinks she's encouraging her spouse, but to him it sounds more like condemnation. But if he has the desire and motivation to seek a better position, her words will bolster his resolve. Until he has that desire, her words will come across as judgmental and guilt-inducing. They express not love but rejection.

If, however, he says, "You know, I've been thinking about starting a handyman business on the side," then she has the opportunity to give words of encouragement. Encouraging words would sound like this. "If you decide to do that, you will be a success. When you set your mind to something, you do it. If that's what you want to do, I will certainly do everything I can to help you." Such words may give him courage to start drawing up a list of potential clients.

Encouragement requires empathy and seeing the world from your spouse's perspective. We must first learn what is important to our spouse. Only then can we give encouragement. With verbal encouragement, we are trying to communicate, "I know. I care. I am with you. How can I help?" We are trying to show we believe in him and in his abilities. We are giving credit and praise.

Most of us have more potential than we will ever develop. What holds us back is often courage. A loving spouse can supply that all-important catalyst. Of course, encouraging words may be difficult for you to speak. It may not be your primary love language. It may take great effort for you to learn this second language. That will be especially true if you have a pattern of critical and condemning words, but I can assure you it will be worth the effort.

What happens when your spouse feels his or her potential has been thwarted? Let's take a look at Jim's story for one example. Jim's wife, Sarah, always called him "The World's Greatest Fighter Pilot" even in public. "I would feel slightly embarrassed when she said it, but secretly I beamed with pride at the same time," he said. "My love language has been words of affirmation from the time I was a child. After my wife and I read *The 5 Love Languages* at a base chapel study, I realized why those positive words were so important. So did my wife. So she began to speak these words of affirmation often and freely, complimenting every act of kindness I did, every good decision I made, and every time I helped her out with the kids."

But all of that changed dramatically when he was passed over for full colonel. "It was the death of a lifelong dream for me and I took it badly," said Jim. "I felt the Air Force was telling me I was not good enough and it hit me hard. I've always struggled with anger, but I grew even angrier than usual after that."

Jim also began to micromanage Sarah's work at home. "I told her how to do the laundry, load the dishwasher, and season the soup," Jim recalled. "My anger got so bad the kids couldn't bring home friends for fear I would blow up. I began to hate the way I was acting, but I justified my actions by blaming the Air Force and becoming bitter toward the military."

It was a vicious circle. When Jim acted unkindly, Sarah found nothing in his behavior to praise or affirm. "It seemed as if my wife's words of affirmation dried up as much as my hope for a future Air Force career dried up," Jim said. When she didn't speak his love language, he didn't speak hers.

At the breaking point of their marriage, they sought counseling with Jim's base chaplain, who encouraged Jim to intentionally speak Sarah's love language (receiving gifts) by writing her cards, bringing home flowers, or picking up little souvenirs for her when Jim went TDY. And he encouraged Sarah to grasp every small opportunity to praise Jim and speak words of affirmation. "At first, it was so hard, because I didn't feel like speaking kind words," said Sarah. "But as I asked God for specific things I could say to encourage my husband, things began to turn around. I'm so thankful for wise counsel that helped me do and say the right things to help restore our marital relationship."

Jim and Sarah's marriage began to regain the traction it once had. "We've been together ten more years since that season of sadness in our lives and it's due to the fact that we expressed love to each other in a love language appropriate way—even during the hard times," said Jim.

Love can be restored when you speak your spouse's love language. Even difficult marriages can change rather quickly when you choose to love, rather than complain.

## KIND WORDS

Love is kind. If then we are to communicate love verbally, we must use kind words. That has to do with the way we speak. The same sentence can have two different meanings, depending on how you say it. Sometimes our words say one thing, but our tone of voice says another. We are sending double messages. Our spouse will usually interpret our message based on our tone of voice, not the words we use.

"I would be delighted to wash dishes tonight," said in a snarling tone will not be received as an expression of love. On the other hand, we can share hurt, pain, and even anger in a kind manner, and that will be an expression of love. "I felt disappointed and hurt that you didn't offer to help me this evening," said in an honest, kind manner can be an expression of love. The person speaking wants to be known by her spouse. She is taking steps to build intimacy by sharing her feelings. She is asking for an opportunity to discuss a hurt in order to find healing. The same words expressed with a loud, harsh voice will be not an expression of love but an expression of condemnation and judgment.

The manner in which we speak is exceedingly important. An ancient sage once said, "A soft answer turns away anger." When your spouse is angry and upset and lashing out words of heat, if you choose to be loving, you will not reciprocate with additional heat but with a soft voice. You will receive what he is saying as information about his emotional feelings. You will let him tell you of his hurt, anger, and perception of events. You will seek to put yourself in his shoes and see the event through his eyes and then express softly and kindly your understanding of why he feels that way. If you have wronged him, you will be willing to confess the wrong and ask forgiveness. If your motivation is different from what he is reading, you will be able to explain your motivation kindly. You will seek understanding and reconciliation, and not to prove your own perception as the only logical way to interpret what has happened. That is mature love—love to which we aspire if we seek a growing marriage.

> ★ ★ ★
>
> I am amazed by how many individuals mess up every new day with yesterday.

Love doesn't keep a score of wrongs. Love doesn't bring up past failures. None of us is perfect. In marriage we do not always do the best or right thing. We have sometimes done and said hurtful things to our spouses. We cannot erase the past. We can only confess it and agree that it was wrong. We can ask for forgiveness and try to act differently in the future. Having confessed my failure and asked forgiveness, I can do nothing more to mitigate the hurt it may have caused my spouse. When I have been wronged by my spouse and she has painfully confessed it and requested forgiveness, I have the option of justice or forgiveness. If I choose justice and seek to pay her back or make her pay for her wrongdoing, I am making myself the judge and she the felon. Intimacy becomes impossible. If, however, I choose to forgive, intimacy can be restored. Forgiveness is the way of love.

I am amazed by how many individuals mess up every new day with yesterday. They insist on bringing into today the failures of yesterday, and in so doing, they pollute a potentially wonderful day. "I can't believe you did it. I don't think I'll ever forget it. You can't possibly know how much you hurt me. I don't know how you can sit there so smugly after you treated me that way. You ought to be crawling on your knees, begging me for forgiveness. I don't know if I can ever forgive you." Those are not the words of love but of bitterness and resentment and revenge.

The best thing we can do with the failures of the past is to let them be history. Yes, it happened. Certainly it hurt. And it may still hurt, but he has acknowledged his failure and asked your forgiveness. We cannot erase the past, but we can accept it as history. We can choose to live today free from the failures of yesterday. Forgiveness is not a feeling; it is a commitment. It's a choice to show mercy, not to hold the offense up against the offender. Forgiveness is an expression of love. "I love you. I care about you, and I choose to forgive you. Even though my feelings of hurt may linger, I will not allow what has happened to come between us. I hope we can learn from this experience. You are not a failure because you have failed. You are my spouse, and together we will go on from here." Those are the words of affirmation expressed in the dialect of kind words.

## HUMBLE WORDS

Love makes requests, not demands. When I demand things from my spouse, I become a parent and she the child. It is the parent who tells the three-year-old what he ought to do and, in fact, what he must do. That is necessary because the three-year-old does not yet know how to navigate in the treacherous waters of life. In marriage, however, we are equal, adult partners. We are not perfect to be sure, but we are adults and we are partners. If we are to develop an intimate relationship, we need to know each other's desires. If we wish to love each other, we need to know what the other person wants.

The way we express those desires, however, is all-important. If they come across as demands, we have erased the possibility of intimacy and will drive our spouse away. If, however, we make our needs and desires known in the form of a request, we are giving guidance, not ultimatums. The husband who says, "Could you make that good pasta one of these nights?" is giving his wife guidance on how to love him and thus build intimacy. On the other hand, the husband who says, "Can't we ever have a decent meal around here?" is being adolescent, is making a demand, and his wife is likely to fire back, "Okay, you cook!" The wife who says, "Do you think it will be possible for you to clean the gutters this weekend?" is expressing love by making a request. But the wife who says, "If you don't get those gutters cleaned out soon, they are going to fall off the house. They already have trees growing out of them!" has ceased to love and has become a domineering spouse.

When you make a request of your spouse, you are affirming his or her worth and abilities. You are in essence indicating she has something or can do something meaningful and worthwhile to you. When, however, you make demands, you have become not a lover but a tyrant. Your spouse will feel not affirmed but belittled. A request introduces the element of choice. Your mate may choose to respond to your request or to deny it, because love is always a choice. That's what makes it meaningful. To know my spouse loves me enough to respond to one of my requests communicates emotionally that she cares about me, respects me, admires me, and wants to do something to please me. We cannot get emotional love by way of demand. My spouse may in fact comply with my demands, but it's not an expression of love. It's an act of fear or guilt or some other emotion, but not love. Thus, a request creates the possibility for an expression of love, whereas a demand suffocates that possibility.

## MORE WAYS TO AFFIRM

Words of affirmation are one of the five basic love languages. Within that language, however, there are many dialects. We have discussed a few already, and there are many more. Entire volumes and numerous articles have been written on these dialects. All of the dialects have in common the use of words to affirm one's spouse. Psychologist William James said that possibly the deepest human need is the need to feel appreciated. Words of affirmation will meet that need in many individuals. If you are not a man or woman of words, if it is not your primary love language but you think it may be the love language of your spouse, let me suggest you keep a notebook titled "Words of Affirmation." When you read an article or book on love, record the words of affirmation you find. When you hear a lecture on love or you overhear a friend saying something positive about another person, write it down. In time, you will collect quite a list of words to use in communicating love to your spouse.

Sometimes you may not know what to say at all. When Terrence came home from war, he processed what he had been through by telling his wife, Lillian, the same stories over and over again. "At first, I wanted him to talk about something else," Lillian remembered. "But when I learned the war experiences were forever a part of who he was, I became a willing listener and a better encourager." By allowing him to share his experiences, Lillian affirmed her husband when he needed it the most. She learned to express appreciation for what he had done. She told him how proud she was of him. Her words were like medicine to his wounded emotions.

You may also want to try giving indirect words of affirmation—that is, saying positive things about your spouse when he or she is not present. Eventually, someone will tell your spouse, and you will get full credit for love. Tell your wife's mother how great your wife is. When her mother tells her what you said, it will be amplified, and you will get even more credit. Also affirm your spouse in front of others when he or she is present. When you are given public honor for an accomplishment, be sure to share the credit with your spouse. You may also try your hand at writing words of affirmation. Written words have the benefit of being read over and over again. While Luke was deployed, he learned his wife, Marlene, treasured his written words of affirmation so much that now, even when he is home, he buys her two or three cards at a time. "I love it!" said Marlene. "I have a rack up in my office where I keep all his cards. I can't tell you how many times I've reread them all."

I learned an important lesson about words of affirmation and love languages years ago in Little Rock, Arkansas. My visit with Bill and Betty Jo was on a beautiful spring day. They lived off base in a cluster home with white picket fence, green grass, and spring flowers in full bloom. It was idyllic. Once inside, however, I discovered the idealism ended. Their marriage was in shambles. Twelve years and two children after the wedding day, they wondered why they had married in the first place. The only thing they really agreed on was that they both loved the children. As the story unfolded, my observation was that Bill was a workaholic who had little time left over for Betty Jo. Betty Jo worked part-time, mainly to get out of the house. Their method of coping was withdrawal. They tried to put distance between themselves so their conflicts would not seem as large. But the gauge on both love tanks read "empty."

They told me they had been going for marriage counseling but didn't seem to be making much progress. They were attending my marriage seminar, and I was leaving town the next day. This would likely be my only encounter with Bill and Betty Jo. I decided to put everything on the table.

I spent an hour with each of them separately. I listened intently to both stories. I discovered that in spite of the emptiness of their relationship and their many disagreements, they appreciated certain things about each other. Bill acknowledged, "She is a good mother. She also is a good housekeeper and an excellent cook when she chooses to cook. But," he continued, "there is simply no affection coming from her. I work my tail off and there is simply no appreciation." In my conversation with Betty Jo, she agreed Bill was an excellent provider. "But," she complained, "he does nothing around the house to help me, and he never has time for me. What's the use of having the house, the recreational vehicle, and all the other things if you don't ever get to enjoy them together?"

With that information, I decided to focus my advice by making only one suggestion to each of them. I told Bill and Betty Jo separately that each one held the key to changing the emotional climate of the marriage. "That key," I said, "is to express verbal appreciation for the things you like about the other person and, for the moment, suspending your complaints about the things you do not like." We reviewed the positive comments they had already made about each other and helped each of them write a list of those positive traits. Bill's list focused on Betty Jo's activities as a mother, housekeeper, and cook. Betty Jo's list focused on Bill's hard work and financial provision of the family. We made the lists as specific as possible. Betty Jo's list included:

• He has received several promotions through the years.
• He is always thinking of ways to improve his productivity.
• He's a good financial manager.
• He bought us a recreational vehicle three years ago.
• He keeps up with the yard work or hires someone to do it.
• He is generous with finances.
• He agrees I can use the money from my part-time job any way I desire.

Bill's list included:

• She keeps our house clean and orderly.
• She cooks dinner about three days a week.
• She buys the groceries.
• She helps the children with their homework.
• She transports the children to school and church activities.
• She teaches first-grade Sunday school.
• She takes my clothes to the cleaners.

I suggested they add to the lists things they noticed in the weeks ahead. I also suggested that twice a week, they select one positive trait and express verbal appreciation for it to the spouse. I gave one further guideline. I told Betty Jo that if Bill happened to give her a compliment, she was not to give him a compliment at the same time, but rather, she should simply receive it and say, "Thank you for saying that." I told

Bill the same thing. I encouraged them to do that every week for two months, and if they found it helpful, they could continue. If the experiment did not help the emotional climate of the marriage, then they could write it off as another failed attempt.

When I called them two months later to check their progress, I spoke to them individually. I was amazed to find Bill's attitude had taken a giant step forward. He loved that she was expressing appreciation for his hard work and his provision for the family. "She has actually made me feel like a man again. We've got a ways to go, Dr. Chapman, but I really believe we are on the road."

When I talked to Betty Jo, however, I found she had only taken a baby step forward. She said, "It has improved some, Dr. Chapman. Bill is giving me verbal compliments as you suggested, and I guess he is sincere. But he's still so busy at work we never spend time together."

As I listened to Betty Jo, the lights came on. I knew I had made a significant discovery. The love language of one person is not necessarily the love language of another. It was obvious Bill's primary love language was Words of Affirmation. What he wanted most from his wife was expressions of appreciation for his work. Betty Jo, on the other hand, was emotionally crying out for something else. That brings us to love language number two.

## YOUR TURN

*Share instances with your spouse when words had a profound impact on your life—positively or negatively.*

## *If your spouse's love language is Words of Affirmation:*

1. To remind yourself that "Words of Affirmation" is your spouse's primary love language, print the following on a 3 x 5 card and put it on a mirror or other place where you will see it daily:

   > Words are important!
   > Words are important!
   > Words are important!

2. For one week, keep a written record of all the words of affirmation you give your spouse each day.

   > On Monday, I said:
   > "You did a great job on this meal."
   > "You really look nice in that outfit."
   > "I appreciate your picking up the dry cleaning."
   >
   > On Tuesday, I said:
   > etc.

   You might be surprised how well (or how poorly) you are speaking words of affirmation.

3. Set a goal to give your spouse a different compliment each day for one month. If "an apple a day keeps the doctor away," maybe a compliment a day will keep the counselor away. (You may want to record these compliments also, so you will not duplicate the statements.)

4. As you watch TV, read, or listen to people's conversations, look for words of affirmation that people use. Write those affirming statements in a notebook or keep them electronically. Read through these periodically and select those you could use with your spouse. When you use one, note the date on which you used it. Your notebook may become your love book. Remember, words are important!

5. Write a love letter, a love paragraph, or a love sentence to your spouse and give it quietly or with fanfare! You may someday find your love letter tucked away in some special place. Words are important!

6. Compliment your spouse in the presence of his parents or friends. You will get double credit: Your spouse will feel loved and the parents will feel lucky to have such a great son-in-law or daughter-in-law.

7. Look for your spouse's strengths and tell her how much you appreciate those strengths. Chances are she will work hard to live up to her reputation.

8. Tell your children how great their mother or father is. Do this behind your spouse's back and in her presence.

---

### Decoding Deployments with Words of Affirmation

Words of Affirmation is one of the easiest languages to speak during separations. In fact, you may find that being intentional with this language will draw the two of you closer together than you thought possible while physically apart.

---

1. Before the deployment, write love notes and secretly tuck them away in various places in the service member's bags. Likewise, the service member can write several cards and label them "For When You're Lonely," "For When You're Overwhelmed," etc., so she can open them when she needs to hear from you the most.

2. Handwrite an encouraging letter to your spouse at least weekly, more often if possible.

3. Remind your spouse of the things that attracted you to her when you first met.

4. Share what you love, admire, or respect about your spouse in a letter or during one of your phone or Internet calls.

5. Write and mail your own poem about your spouse.

6. Express appreciation. Service members, tell your spouse how much you appreciate all the things she does to keep the homefront going.

7. Home front spouse, be sure your service member still feels needed by your family, no matter how well you are managing without him.

8. If your spouse is stressed when he or she calls you, allow him the opportunity to vent. Don't try to fix the situation unless asked. Affirm him or her.

9. Write and send a tribute to your spouse.

10. Be the first to say "I love you" in every conversation.

# THE 5 LOVE LANGUAGES®

# CHAPTER 5

LOVE LANGUAGE #2

# Quality Time

I should have picked up on Betty Jo's primary love language from the beginning. What was she saying on that spring night when I visited her and Bill in Little Rock? "Bill is a good provider, but he doesn't spend any time with me. What good are all our things if we don't ever enjoy them together?" What was her desire? Quality time with Bill. She wanted his attention. She wanted him to focus on her, to give her time, to do things with her.

By "quality time," I mean giving someone your undivided attention. I don't mean sitting on the couch watching television together. When you spend time that way, ABC or HBO has your attention—not your spouse. What I mean is sitting on the couch with the TV off, looking at each other and talking, giving each other your undivided attention. It means taking a walk, just the two of you, or going out to eat and looking at each other and talking. Have you ever noticed that in a restaurant, you can almost always tell the difference between a dating couple and a married couple? Dating couples look at each other and talk. Married couples sit there and gaze around the restaurant. You'd think they went there to eat!

When I sit with my wife and give her twenty minutes of my undivided attention and she does the same for me, we are giving each other twenty minutes of life. We will never have those twenty minutes again; we are giving our lives to each other. It's a powerful emotional communicator of love.

One medicine cannot cure all diseases. In my advice to Bill and Betty Jo, I made a serious mistake. I assumed words of affirmation would mean as much to Betty Jo as they would to Bill. I had hoped that if each of them would give adequate verbal affirmation, the emotional climate would change, and both of them would begin to feel loved. It worked for Bill. He began to feel more positive about Betty Jo. He began to sense genuine appreciation for his hard work, but it had not worked as well for Betty Jo, for words of affirmation was not her primary love language. Her language was quality time.

I got back on the phone and thanked Bill for his efforts in the past two months verbally affirming Betty Jo. "But, Dr. Chapman," he said, "she is still not very happy."

"I think I know why," I said. "The problem is that I suggested the wrong love language." Bill hadn't the foggiest idea what I meant. I explained that what makes one person feel loved emotionally is not always the thing that makes another person feel loved emotionally.

I explained that Betty Jo's language was not words of affirmation but quality time. I explained the concept of giving someone your undivided attention, doing something with her that she enjoys doing and doing it wholeheartedly. "Like going to the symphony with her," he said. I could tell the lights were coming on in Little Rock.

"Dr. Chapman, that's what she has always complained about. I didn't do things with her, I didn't spend any time with her. 'We used to go places and do things before we were married,' she said, 'but now, you're too busy.' That's her love language all right. But what am I gonna do? My job is so demanding."

"Tell me about it," I said.

For the next ten minutes, he gave me the history of his climb up the organizational ladder, of how hard he had worked, and how proud he was of his accomplishments. He told me of his dreams for the future and that he knew that within the next five years, he would be where he wanted to be.

"Do you want to be there alone, or do you want to be there with Betty Jo and the children?" I asked.

"I want her to be with me, Dr. Chapman. I want her to enjoy it with me. That's why it always hurts so much when she criticizes me for spending time on the job. I am doing it for us. I wanted her to be a part of it, but she is always so negative."

"Are you beginning to see why she was so negative, Bill?" I asked. "Her love language is quality time. You have given her so little time that her love tank is empty. She doesn't feel secure in your love. Therefore she has lashed out at what was taking your time in her mind—your job. She doesn't really hate your job. She hates the fact that she feels so little love coming from you. There's only one answer, Bill, and it's costly. You have to make time for Betty Jo. You have to love her in the right love language."

"I know you are right, Dr. Chapman. Where do I begin?"

"Let's make another list. What are some things you know Betty Jo would like you to do with her? Things she has mentioned through the years." Bill's list included:

- Spend a weekend in the mountains (sometimes with the children and sometimes just the two of us).
- Meet her for lunch (at a nice restaurant or sometimes even at McDonald's).
- Get a babysitter and take her out to dinner, just the two of us.
- When I come home at night, sit down and talk with her about my day and listen as she tells me about her day. (She doesn't want me to watch TV while we are trying to talk.)
- Spend time with the children.
- Take a vacation with the family at least once a year.
- Go walking with her and talk as we walk.

"Those are the things she has talked about through the years," he said.

"You know what I am going to suggest, don't you, Bill?"

"Do them," he said.

"That's right, one a week for the next two months. Where will you find the time? You will make it. You are a wise man," I continued. "You would not be where you are if you were not a good decision maker. You have the ability to plan your life and to include Betty Jo in your plans."

"I know," he said. "I can do it."

"And, Bill, this does not have to diminish your vocational goals. It just means when you get to the top, Betty Jo and the children will be with you."

"That's what I want more than anything. Whether I am at the top or not, I want her to be happy, and I want to enjoy life with her and the children."

The years have come and gone. Bill and Betty Jo have gone to the top and back, but the important thing is they have done it together. The children have left the nest, and Bill and Betty Jo agree these are their best years ever. Bill has become an avid symphony fan, and Betty Jo has made an unending list in her legal pad of things she appreciates about Bill. He never tires of hearing them. He has now started his own company and is near the top again. His job is no longer a threat to Betty Jo. She is excited about it and encourages him. She knows she is number one in his life. Her love tank is full, and if it begins to get empty, she knows a simple request on her part will get her Bill's undivided attention.

## FOCUSED ATTENTION

It isn't enough to just be in the same room with someone. A key ingredient in giving your spouse quality time is giving them focused attention, especially in this era of many distractions. When a father is sitting on the floor, rolling a ball to his two-year-old, his attention is not focused on the ball but on his child. For that brief moment, however long it lasts, they are together. If, however, the father is talking on the phone while he rolls the ball, his attention is diluted. Some husbands and wives think they are spending time together when, in reality, they are only living in close proximity. They are in the same house at the same time, but they are not together. A wife who is texting while her husband tries to talk to her is not giving him quality time, because he does not have her full attention.

Quality time does not mean we have to spend our together moments gazing into each other's eyes. It means we are doing something together and we are giving our full attention to the other person. The activity in which we are both engaged is incidental. The important thing emotionally is that we are spending focused time with each other. The activity is a vehicle that creates the sense of togetherness. The important thing about the father rolling the ball to the two-year-old is not the activity itself but the emotions that are created between the father and his child.

Similarly, a husband and wife playing tennis together, if it's genuine quality time, will focus not on the game but on the fact that they are spending time together. What happens on the emotional level is what matters. Our spending time together in a common pursuit communicates that we care about each other, that we enjoy being with each other, that we like to do things together.

## QUALITY TIMING

For those whose primary love language is quality time, the military lifestyle presents special challenges. Demanding schedules require intentionality. Timing is key. Service members, be aware that with each PCS, the fresh absence of friends from your last station will further deplete the love tanks of those whose love language is quality time. Investing in one-on-one time with your spouse during these times will reassure him or her of your love, and help ease the transition.

While the need for quality time may be felt more keenly in new environments, this is not a love language you can ever put on hold without risking harm to your relationship. Obviously, deployments are difficult (tips for coping with them are at the end of this chapter). But even while stateside, job pressures can threaten to squeeze out quality time with one's spouse. During the Gulf War in 1991, Ted was a battalion chaplain, responsible for processing soldiers headed to Iraq. "This was during a time when they projected that thirty thousand of our soldiers would be killed in the first month of the war," said Ted. "There was a lot of fear about down range, and I was trying to be a super chaplain." While Ted took calls and met with soldiers at all hours of the day and night, his wife, Penny, was earning a master's degree and raising two small children. They both worked hard, but had little time for each other.

In January, Ted began to make plans for Valentine's Day to make up for months of long hours. So he arranged for child care, made reservations at a nice restaurant and hotel, and purchased lingerie at Victoria's Secret for Penny. Valentine's Day arrived, and the date went well—until Penny opened the gift.

As she lifted the lingerie out of the tissue paper, her face fell. "Oh. Thank you," was all she said.

"That reaction reached into my chest, pulled my heart out and threw it on the floor and stomped on it," Ted said. "I thought, 'She doesn't love me.'"

For three weeks, Ted and Penny felt cold and distant to each other, until finally, Ted decided to address what was bothering him. Her explanation shocked him. "When I opened your gift, I thought the only thing you liked about me was sex," she told him. The evening had felt like quality time to Penny only until she guessed it was only a way to meet Ted's desire for physical touch.

"That was a totally foreign concept to me, but I had enough wisdom to realize it didn't matter what I thought," Ted said. "It mattered what she thought. I realized I had better figure out how to show her I love her in a way that she understands."

Since then, Ted and Penny have carved out time for regular dates, rather than waiting for the right moment and then splurging on a more expensive night out. "There's far less tension between us now," said Ted. "In fact, if Penny and I started fighting, the kids would tell us to go on a date!" Even the children knew Penny's love language was quality time. When Penny's love tank is full, she's far more willing to speak Ted's love language, as well.

Ted and Penny's relationship demonstrates the connection between love and sex. Without love, the sexual relationship may be extremely empty. Keeping your spouse's love tank full will also enhance your sexual relationship.

In their first year of marriage, Maria understood that her need for quality time with her husband, Jorge, took a backseat to Jorge's responsibilities to the military. For weeks, she looked forward to being together again. But when Jorge came home from sea and immediately began making plans to visit friends, she was crushed—and angry.

"I'm an extrovert," said Jorge. "And when I come home from being underway, I relax by getting together with friends. Maria is always welcome to be part of the group, but sometimes she chooses not to. If she wants to be with me so much, why would she stay home?"

Maria didn't want to be part of a group. She wanted his focused attention to reassure her of his love. "If we could have some quality time together first, just us, I'd be much happier for him to see his friends. But when he asks to do something with them right away, I wonder if he even missed me while he was gone."

Maria is clearly revealing that her love language is quality time. That is why she finds Jorge's desire to spend time with his friends as an act of rejection. If Jorge is wise, he will fill Maria's love tank before he dashes off to see his friends.

Quality time is critical and should be carefully timed—but unfortunately, it cannot be stored up like water in a camel's hump, ready to be used on a journey through the desert. Connor was already gone from home on a TDY when he learned of an upcoming deployment with the National Guard. So he flew home every weekend to spend quality time with his wife, Susan. Each weekend was to be spent without distractions of the Internet, email, texting, webcam, or TV.

"It was a tall order for anyone to fill, especially under such difficult circumstances, but he longed to spend quality time with me, to have my undivided attention," remembered Susan, who contributes to an online support group for military wives. "So each weekend, we read together, prayed together, listened to the Gary and Barb Rosberg pre-deployment DVDs, completed a barrage of home repairs, and spent time preparing our four children, as best we could, for our next assignment. He even went out of his way to sit next to me, as I wrote blogs and devotionals, like he used to do before his TDY."

——— ★ ★ ★ ———

Most individuals who complain that their spouse does not talk do not mean literally that he or she never says a word.

But the fact that Susan spent any time on the blogs for military wives hurt Connor. "His heart was crushed by my inability to give him the undivided attention he needed," she said. "Through his eyes, my priorities were displaced. He no longer affirmed my writing, and he struggled to find the encouraging words I so desperately longed to hear. As a result, I struggled to express my heart, physically, verbally, and in writing. To make matters worse, there was no time to process the feelings and emotions that surfaced before he had to leave again on his yearlong deployment."

Connor is demonstrating a common source of conflict. He was making great efforts to meet his own emotional need for love, probably assuming he was also meeting Susan's need for love. When he did not get the quality time he thought he deserved, he became critical of Susan. Her love language was words of affirmation, so she felt deeply hurt by his negative words. So, another couple starts a long deployment with a fractured relationship.

Connor's expectations were unrealistic. He was trying to "load up" on enough quality time to see him through deployment. The truth is that quality time cannot be stored up. However, we can speak quality time while deployed. (See suggestions at the end of this chapter.)

## QUALITY CONVERSATION

Like words of affirmation, the language of quality time also has many dialects. One of the most common dialects is that of *quality conversation*. By quality conversation, I mean sympathetic dialogue where two individuals are sharing their experiences, thoughts, feelings, and desires in a friendly, uninterrupted context. Most individuals who complain that their spouse does not talk do not mean literally that he or she never says a word. They mean that he or she seldom takes part in sympathetic dialogue. If your spouse's primary love language is quality time, such dialogue is crucial to his or her emotional sense of being loved.

Quality conversation is quite different from the first love language. Words of affirmation focus on what we are saying, whereas quality conversation focuses on what we are hearing. If I am sharing my love for you by means of quality time and we are going to spend that time in conversation, it means I will focus on drawing you out, listening sympathetically to what you have to say. I will ask questions, not in a badgering manner but with a genuine desire to understand your thoughts, feelings, and desires.

★ ★ ★

"She didn't want advice; she just wanted to know I understood."

I met Patrick when he was forty-three and had been married for seventeen years. He sat in the leather chair in my office, and after briefly introducing himself, he leaned forward and said with great emotion, "Dr. Chapman, I have been a fool, a real fool."

"What has led you to that conclusion?" I asked.

"I've been married for seventeen years," he said, "and my wife has left me. Now I realize what a fool I've been."

I repeated my original question, "In what way have you been a fool?"

"My wife would come home from work and tell me about the problems in her office. I'd listen to her and then tell her what I thought she should do. I advised her to confront the problem. 'Problems don't go away. You have to talk with the people involved or your supervisor.' The next day she would come home from work and tell me about the same problems. I would ask her if she did what I had suggested the day before. She hadn't. So I'd repeat my advice. She would come home the next day and tell me about the same problems. Again I would ask her if she had done what I had suggested. She would shake her head and say no.

"After three or four nights of that, I got angry. I told her not to expect any sympathy from me if she wasn't willing to take my advice. It hurt me to see her living under such stress because I knew she didn't have to. The next time she'd bring up the problem, I said, 'If you're not going to listen to my advice, I don't want to hear it.'

"What a fool I was," he said, "what a fool! Now I realize she didn't want advice when she told me about her struggles at work. She wanted sympathy. She wanted me to listen, to give her attention, to let her know I could understand the hurt, the stress, the pressure. She wanted to know I loved her and I was with her. She didn't want advice; she just wanted to know I understood. But I never tried to understand. I was too busy giving advice. What a fool. And now she is gone."

Patrick's wife had been pleading for quality conversation. Emotionally, she longed for him to focus attention on her by listening to her pain and frustration. Patrick was not focusing on listening but on speaking. He listened only long enough to hear the problem and formulate a solution. He didn't listen long enough or well enough to hear her cry for support and understanding.

Many of us are like Patrick. We are trained to analyze problems and create solutions. We forget that marriage is a relationship, not a project to be completed or a problem to solve. A relationship calls for sympathetic listening with a view to understanding the other person's thoughts, feelings, and desires. We must be willing to give advice but only when it's requested and never in a condescending manner. Most of us have little training in listening. We are far more efficient in thinking and speaking. Learning to listen may be as difficult as learning a foreign language, but learn we must, if we want to communicate love. That is especially true if your spouse's primary love language is quality time and his or her dialect is quality conversation. Fortunately, numerous books and articles have been written on developing the art of listening. I will not seek to repeat what is written elsewhere but suggest the following summary of practical tips.

1. Maintain eye contact when your spouse is talking. That keeps your mind from wandering and communicates that he/she has your full attention.

2. Don't listen to your spouse and do something else at the same time. Remember, quality time is giving someone your undivided attention. If you are doing something you cannot turn from immediately, tell your spouse the truth. A positive approach might be, "I know you are trying to talk to me and I'm interested, but I want to give you my full attention. I can't do that right now, but if

you will give me ten minutes to finish this, I'll sit down and listen to you." Most spouses will respect such a request.

3. Listen for feelings. Ask yourself, "What emotion is my spouse experiencing?" When you think you have the answer, confirm it. For example, "It sounds to me like you are feeling disappointed because I forgot _____." That gives him the chance to clarify his feelings. It also communicates you are listening intently to what he is saying.

4. Observe body language. Clenched fists, trembling hands, tears, furrowed brows, and eye movement may give you clues as to what the other is feeling. Sometimes body language speaks one message while words speak another. Ask for clarification to make sure you know what she is really thinking and feeling.

5. Refuse to interrupt. Recent research has indicated that the average individual listens for only seventeen seconds before interrupting and interjecting his own ideas. If I give you my undivided attention while you are talking, I will refrain from defending myself or hurling accusations at you or dogmatically stating my position. My goal is to discover your thoughts and feelings. My objective is not to defend myself or to set you straight. It is to understand you.

## LEARNING TO TALK

Quality conversation requires not only sympathetic listening but also self-revelation. When a wife says, "I wish my husband would talk. I never know what he's thinking or feeling," she is pleading for intimacy.

She wants to feel close to her husband, but how can she feel close to someone whom she doesn't know? In order for her to feel loved, he must learn to reveal himself. If her primary love language is quality time and her dialect is quality conversation, her emotional love tank will never be filled until he tells her his thoughts and feelings.

Self-revelation does not come easy for some of us. Many adults grew up in homes where the expression of thoughts and feelings was not encouraged but condemned. To request a toy was to receive a lecture on the sad state of family finances. The child went away feeling guilty for having the desire, and he quickly learned not to express his desires. When he expressed anger, the parents responded with harsh and condemning words. Thus, the child learned that expressing angry feelings is not appropriate. If the child was made to feel guilty for expressing disappointment at not being able to go to the store with his father, he learned to hold his disappointment inside. By the time we reach adulthood, many of us have learned to deny our feelings. We are no longer in touch with our emotional selves.

A wife says to her husband, "How did you feel about what Steve did?" And the husband responds, "I think he was wrong. He should have—" but he is not telling her his feelings. He is voicing his thoughts. Perhaps he has reason to feel angry, hurt, or disappointed, but he has lived so long in the world of thought that he does not acknowledge his feelings. When he decides to learn the language of quality conversation, it will be like learning a foreign language. The place to begin is by getting in touch with his feelings, becoming aware that he is an emotional creature in spite of the fact that he has denied that part of his life.

If you need to learn the language of quality conversation, begin by noting the emotions you feel away from home. Carry a small notepad and keep it with you daily. Three times each day, ask yourself, "What emotions have I felt in the last three hours? What did I feel on the way to work when the driver behind me was riding my bumper? What did I feel when I stopped at the gas station and the automatic pump did not shut off and the side of the car was covered in gas? What did I feel when I got to the office and found that the project I was working on had to be completed in three days when I thought I had another two weeks?"

Write down your feelings in the notepad and a word or two to help you remember the event corresponding to the feeling. Your list may look like this:

| **Event** | **Feelings** |
| --- | --- |
| • tailgater | • angry |
| • gas station | • very upset |
| • work project due in three days | • frustrated and anxious |

Do that exercise three times a day and you will develop an awareness of your emotional nature. Using your notepad, communicate your emotions and the events briefly with your spouse as many days as possible. In a few weeks, you will become comfortable expressing your emotions with him or her. And eventually you will feel comfortable discussing your emotions toward your spouse and the children, stimulated by events that occur within the home. Remember, emotions themselves are neither good nor bad. They are simply our psychological responses to the events of life.

Based on our thoughts and emotions, we eventually make decisions. When the tailgater was following you on the highway and you felt angry, perhaps you had these thoughts: I wish he would lay off; I wish he would pass me; if I thought I wouldn't get caught, I'd press the accelerator and leave him in the twilight; I should slam on my brakes and let his insurance company buy me a new car; maybe I'll pull off the road and let him pass.

Eventually, you made some decision or the other driver backed off, turned, or passed you, and you arrived safely at work. In each of life's events, we have emotions, thoughts, desires, and eventually actions. It is the expression of that process we call self-revelation. If you choose to learn the love dialect of quality conversation, that is the learning road you must follow.

## DEAD SEAS AND BABBLING BROOKS

Not all of us are out of touch with our emotions, but when it comes to talking, all of us are affected by our personality. I have observed two basic personality types. The first I call the "Dead Sea." In the little nation of Israel, the Sea of Galilee flows south by way of the Jordan River into the Dead Sea. The Dead Sea goes nowhere. It receives but it does not give. This personality type receives many experiences, emotions, and thoughts throughout the day. They have a large reservoir where they store that information, and they are perfectly happy not to talk. If you say to a Dead Sea personality, "What's wrong? Why aren't you talking tonight?" he will probably answer, "Nothing's wrong. What makes you think something's wrong?" And that response is perfectly honest. He is content not to talk. He could drive from Chicago to Detroit and never say a word and be perfectly happy.

On the other extreme is the "Babbling Brook." For this personality, whatever enters into the eye gate or the ear gate comes out the mouth gate and there are seldom sixty seconds between the two. Whatever they see, whatever they hear, they tell. In fact if no one is at home to talk to, they will call someone else. "Do you know what I saw? Do you know what I heard?" If they can't get someone on the telephone, they may talk to themselves because they have no reservoir. Many times a Dead Sea marries a Babbling Brook. That happens because when they are dating, it's a very attractive match.

If you are a Dead Sea and you date a Babbling Brook, you will have a wonderful evening. You don't have to think, "How will I get the conversation started tonight? How will I keep the conversation flowing?" In fact, you don't have to think at all. All you have to do is nod your head and say, "Uh-huh," and she will fill up the whole evening and you will go home saying, "What a wonderful person." On the other hand, if you are a Babbling Brook and you date a Dead Sea, you will have an equally wonderful evening because Dead Seas are the world's best listeners. You will babble for three hours. He will listen intently to you, and you will go home saying, "What a wonderful person." You attract each other. But five years after marriage, the Babbling Brook wakes up one morning and says, "We've been married five years, and I don't know him." The Dead Sea is saying, "I know her too well. I wish she would stop the flow and give me a break." The good news is that Dead Seas can learn to talk and Babbling Brooks can learn to listen. We are influenced by our personality but not controlled by it.

One way to learn new patterns is to establish a daily sharing time in which each of you will talk about three things that happened to you that day and how you feel about them. I call that the "Minimum Daily Requirement" for a healthy marriage. If you will start with the daily minimum, in a few weeks or months you may find quality conversation flowing more freely between you.

## QUALITY ACTIVITIES

In addition to the basic love language of quality time, or giving your spouse your undivided attention, is another dialect called quality activities. At a recent marriage seminar, I asked couples to complete the following sentence: "I feel most loved by my husband/wife when _____." Here is the response of a twenty-nine-year-old husband who has been married for eight years: "I feel most loved by my wife when we do things together, things I like to do and things she likes to do. We talk more. It sorta feels like we are dating again." That is a typical response of individuals whose primary love language is quality time. The emphasis is on being together, doing things together, giving each other undivided attention.

Quality activities may include anything in which one or both of you have an interest. The emphasis is not on what you are doing but on why you are doing it. The purpose is to experience something together, to walk away from it feeling "He cares about me. He was willing to do something with me that I enjoy, and he did it with a positive attitude." That is love, and for some people it is love's loudest voice.

Quality activities may include such activities as putting in a garden, visiting historic neighborhoods, shopping for antiques, going to a concert, taking long walks, or having another couple over for homemade soup and bread. The activities are limited only by your interest and willingness to try new experiences. The essential ingredients in a quality activity are: (1) at least one of you wants to do it, (2) the other is willing to do it, (3) both of you know why you are doing it—to express love by being together.

One of the by-products of quality activities is that they provide a memory bank from which to draw in the years ahead. Fortunate is the couple who remembers an early morning stroll along the coast, the spring they planted the flower garden, the time they got poison ivy chasing the rabbit through the woods, the night they attended their first major-league baseball game together, the one and only time they went skiing together and he broke his leg, the amusement parks, the concerts, the cathedrals, and oh yes, the awe of standing beneath the waterfall after the two-mile hike. They can almost feel the mist as they remember. Those are memories of love, especially for the person whose primary love language is quality time.

And where do we find time for such activities, especially if both of us have vocations outside the home? We make time just as we make time for lunch and dinner. Why? Because it's just as essential to our marriage as meals are to our health. Is it difficult? Does it take careful planning? Yes. Does it mean we have to give up some individual activities? Perhaps. Does it mean we do some things we don't particularly enjoy? Certainly. Is it worth it? Without a doubt. What's in it for me? The pleasure of living with a spouse who feels loved and knowing I have learned to speak his or her love language fluently.

## YOUR TURN

*What in your marriage detracts from spending quality time?*

### *If your spouse's love language is Quality Time:*

1. Take a walk together through the old neighborhood where one of you grew up. Ask questions about your spouse's childhood. Ask, "What are the fun memories of your childhood?" Then, "What was most painful about your childhood?"
2. Go to the city park and rent bicycles. Ride until you are tired, then sit and watch the ducks. When you get tired of the quacks, roll on to the rose garden. Learn each other's favorite color of rose and why.

3. Ask your spouse for a list of five activities he would enjoy doing with you. Make plans to do one of them each month for the next five months. If money is a problem, space the freebies between the "we can't afford this" events.

4. Ask your spouse where she most enjoys sitting when talking with you. The next week, text her one afternoon and say, "I want to make a date with you one evening this week to sit on the porch and talk. Which night and what time would be best for you?"

5. Think of an activity your spouse enjoys, but which brings little pleasure to you: NASCAR, browsing in flea markets, working out. Tell your spouse you are trying to broaden your horizons and would like to join him in this activity sometime this month. Set a date and give it your best effort.

6. Plan a weekend getaway just for the two of you sometime within the next six months. Be sure it's a weekend when you won't have to call the office or have a commitment with your kids. Focus on relaxing together doing what one or both of you enjoy.

7. Make time every day to share with each other some of the events of the day. When you spend more time watching the news than you do listening to each other, you end up more concerned about the Middle East than about your spouse. Or: When you spend more time on Facebook than you do listening to each other, you end up more concerned about your hundreds of "friends" than about your spouse.

8. Have a "Let's review our history" evening once every three months. Set aside an hour to focus on your history. Select five questions each of you will answer, such as:

(1) Who was your best and worst teacher in school and why?
(2) When did you feel your parents were proud of you?
(3) What is the worst mistake your mother ever made?
(4) What is the worst mistake your father ever made?
(5) What do you remember about the religious aspect of your childhood?

Each evening, agree on your five questions before you begin your sharing. At the end of the five questions, stop and decide upon the five questions you will ask next time.

9. Camp out in the living room. Spread your blankets and pillows on the floor. Get your Pepsi and popcorn. Pretend the TV is broken and talk like you used to when you were dating. Talk till the sun comes up or something else happens. If the floor gets too hard, go back upstairs and go to bed. You won't forget this evening!

## Decoding Deployments with Quality Time

Those whose primary love language is Quality Time will naturally feel their love tanks being depleted during deployments. You may want to ramp up his or her second most dominant love language to help, but there are still several ways to experience quality time across the miles.

1. Create your own website together. Post all your news and latest photos weekly for your sweetheart. Write a daily (or as often as possible) online journal to keep your loved one up-to-date.

2. Keep a phone journal. Jot down things you want to tell your spouse when he/she calls. Rule of thumb: always say "I love you" before anything else, just in case you lose connection.

3. Plan dates for a Skype chat when possible. When the technology won't support that, spend quality time writing intentional emails or letters to one another. Your spouse will appreciate the time you invest in any form of communication.

4. Plan a "date" with your spouse to meet at a predesignated website and read a short article and discuss it over the phone or Internet call.

5. "Meet" at a predesignated website that describes a vacation destination you would like to go to when he returns from his deployment.

6. Read a book together; a chapter per week and discuss it the next time you talk with each other. If that is too much of a time commitment, select questions to answer from *101 Conversation Starters for Couples*.

7. Service member, remember your spouse wants to connect on a heart level despite the distance. If you can't or would rather not share what's going on at your end, at least share with her how you feel. Tired? Overwhelmed? Hopeful? Laser-focused?

8. Ask your spouse to share his or her dreams with you. Try not to minimize them in any way. Just listen and show interest.

9. Home front spouse, become interested in a sport, hobby, or activity your service member enjoys. Share what you are learning. You

might even consider taking a few lessons to help you engage with your spouse in this activity when he or she returns.

10. Make a scrapbook of things that took place while the service member was away. You'll spend quality time reliving the memories with him or her after homecoming.

11. Dream together about what you want to do after retirement from the military.

12. Tell your spouse things like, "I can't wait to spend a day ____ with you again." Fill in the blank with a favorite shared activity.

# THE 5 LOVE LANGUAGES®

# CHAPTER 6

LOVE LANGUAGE #3

# Receiving Gifts

I was in Chicago when I studied anthropology. By means of detailed ethnographies (printed descriptions of a particular culture), I visited fascinating peoples all over the world. I went to Central America and studied the advanced cultures of the Mayans and the Aztecs. I crossed the Pacific and studied the tribal peoples of Melanesia and Polynesia. I studied the Eskimos of the northern tundra and the aboriginal Ainus of Japan. I examined the cultural patterns surrounding love and marriage and found that in every culture I studied, gift giving was a part of the love-marriage process.

Anthropologists are intrigued by cultural patterns that tend to pervade cultures, and so was I. Could it be that gift giving is a fundamental expression of love that transcends cultural barriers? Is the attitude of love always accompanied by the concept of giving? Those are academic and somewhat philosophical questions, but if the answer is yes, it has profound practical implications for North American couples.

## "JUICE FOR YOU"

I took an anthropology field trip to the island of Dominica. Our purpose was to study the culture of the Carib Indians, and on the trip I met Fred. Fred was not a Carib but a young black man of twenty-eight years. Fred had lost a hand in a fishing-by-dynamite accident. Since the accident, he could not continue his fishing career. He had plenty of available time, and I welcomed his companionship. We spent hours together talking about his culture.

Upon my first visit to Fred's house, he said to me, "Mr. Gary, would you like to have some juice?" to which I responded enthusiastically. He turned to his younger brother and said, "Go get Mr. Gary some juice." His brother turned, walked down the dirt path, climbed a coconut tree, and returned with a green coconut. "Open it," Fred commanded. With three swift movements of the machete, his brother uncorked the coconut, leaving a triangular hole at the top. Fred handed me the coconut and said, "Juice for you." It was green, but I drank it—all of it—because I knew it was a gift of love. I was his friend, and to friends you give juice.

At the end of our weeks together as I prepared to leave that small island, Fred gave me a final token of his love. It was a crooked stick fourteen inches in length that he had taken from the ocean. It was silky smooth from pounding upon the rocks. Fred said the stick had lived on the shores of Dominica for a long time, and he wanted me to have it as a reminder of the beautiful island. Even today when I look at that stick, I can almost hear the sound of the Caribbean waves, but it's not as much a reminder of Dominica as it is a reminder of love.

A gift is something you can hold in your hand and say, "Look, he was thinking of me," or, "She remembered me." You must be thinking of someone to give him a gift. The gift itself is a symbol of that thought. It doesn't matter whether it costs money. What is important is that you thought of him. And it's not the thought implanted only in the mind that counts, but the thought expressed in actually securing the gift and giving it as the expression of love.

Mothers remember the days their children bring a flower from the yard as a gift. They feel loved, even if it was a flower they didn't want picked. From early years, children are inclined to give gifts to their parents, which may be another indication that gift giving is fundamental to love.

Gifts are visual symbols of love. Most wedding ceremonies include the giving and receiving of rings. The person performing the ceremony says, "These rings are outward and visible signs of an inward and spiritual bond uniting your two hearts in love that has no end." That is not meaningless rhetoric. It is verbalizing a significant truth—symbols have emotional value. Perhaps that is even more graphically displayed near the end of a disintegrating marriage when the husband or wife stops wearing the wedding ring. It's a visual sign that the marriage is in serious trouble.

Visual symbols of love are more important to some people than to others. If receiving gifts is my primary love language, I will place great value on the ring you have given me and I will wear it with great pride. I will also be greatly moved emotionally by other gifts that you give through the years. I will see them as expressions of love. Without gifts as visual symbols, I may question your love.

When Davis and Anna married, they were so poor they used plain 10K gold rings Anna's parents had bought them. Within ten years, they had paid off all their debt, had money in savings, and even were able to purchase a replacement class ring for Davis, which cost several thousand dollars. "But he didn't splurge on a nice ring for me," said Anna. "This was problematic. Every time I looked at my girlfriends' left ring finger, I saw a diamond. But when I looked at my own, I saw a plain gold band." For Anna, whose love language is receiving gifts, that seemed to shout that she just wasn't worth a diamond.

"After five kids, ten years of marriage, and nine military moves, I felt I wanted that demonstration of love on my finger," Anna recalled. Finally, she talked to Davis about it and tried to explain her love language without sounding materialistic.

Not long after that conversation, a set of Anna's grandmother's heirloom china dishes were stolen from their household goods during a move. When the settlement check came in, it provided some discretionary funds. For their tenth anniversary, Davis gave Anna a diamond anniversary band with ten stones to replace the plain gold band. "For the last fifteen years (we are celebrating our twenty-fifth anniversary this year), every time I look down at my ring finger, I feel loved by my military man," Anna said.

★ ★ ★

If you are to become an effective gift giver, you may have to change your attitude about money.

Gifts come in all sizes, colors, and shapes. Some are expensive, and others are free. To the individual whose primary love language is receiving gifts, the cost of the gift will matter little, unless it is greatly out of line with what you can afford. If a millionaire gives only one-dollar gifts regularly, the spouse may question whether that is an expression of love, but when family finances are limited, a one-dollar gift may speak a million dollars worth of love.

Gifts may be purchased, found, or made. The husband who finds an interesting bird feather while out jogging and brings it home to his wife has found himself an expression of love, unless, of course, his wife is allergic to feathers. For the man who can afford it, you can purchase a beautiful card for less than five dollars. For the man who cannot, you can make one for free. Get the paper out of the trash can where you work, fold it in the middle, take scissors and cut out a heart, write "I love you," and sign your name. Gifts need not be expensive.

But what of the person who says, "I'm not a gift giver. I didn't receive many gifts growing up. I never learned how to select gifts. It doesn't come naturally for me." Congratulations, you have just made the first discovery in becoming a great lover. You and your spouse speak different love languages. Now that you have made that discovery, get on with the business of learning your second language. If your spouse's primary love language is receiving gifts, you can become a proficient gift giver. In fact, it's one of the easiest love languages to learn.

Where do you begin? Make a list of all the gifts your spouse has expressed excitement about receiving through the years. They may be gifts you have given or gifts given by other family members or friends. The list will give you an idea of the kind of gifts your spouse would enjoy receiving. If you have little or no knowledge about selecting the kinds of gifts on your list, recruit the help of family members who know your spouse. In the meantime, select gifts you feel comfortable purchasing, making, or finding, and give them to your spouse. Don't wait for a special occasion. If receiving gifts is his/her primary love language, almost anything you give will be received as an expression of love. (If she has been critical of your gifts in the past and almost nothing you have given has been acceptable, then receiving gifts is almost certainly not her primary love language.)

## THE BEST INVESTMENT

If you are to become an effective gift giver, you may have to change your attitude about money. Each of us has an individualized perception of the purposes of money, and we have various emotions associated with spending it. Some of us have a spending orientation. We feel good about ourselves when we are spending money. Others have a saving and investing perspective. We feel good about ourselves when we are saving money and investing it wisely.

If you are a spender, you will have little difficulty purchasing gifts for your spouse; but if you are a saver, you will experience emotional resistance to the idea of spending money as an expression of love. You don't purchase things for yourself. Why should you purchase things for your spouse? But that attitude fails to recognize that you are purchasing things for yourself. By saving and investing money, you are purchasing self-worth and emotional security. You are caring for your own emotional needs in the way you handle money. What you are not doing is meeting the emotional needs of your spouse.

Rachel was raised in a dysfunctional home. Instead of the hoped-for son, she was the second daughter. As such, she was often overlooked and neglected. Though she didn't know it at the time, her love language was receiving gifts, which explains why it hurt so much when her parents gave her a combination birthday/Christmas gift (her birthday is December 28), and it ended up being the same gift her sister received for Christmas. When she graduated from high school, the only child of three to do so, her parents gave her a necklace. "They bragged that they bought the pearls at a garage sale for only one dollar and it turned out they were real," said Rachel. "They weren't. The cheap veneer wore off eventually to reveal the plastic beads beneath. Nothing was too cheap for me."

When Rachel married her Air Force pilot, Trent, they read *The 5 Love Languages* in a base chapel Sunday school class, and it explained why gifts were so important to her. Trent, whose love language was words of affirmation, didn't understand. "I felt that speaking a kind word was a lot easier than going out to buy a gift," he said. So he didn't speak Rachel's language on a regular basis for years.

Finally, Rachel asked him, "What if I only said 'thank you' to you once every other month? Even after you've done a lot of work around the house, or ran an errand for me, I rarely said 'thank you.' How would that make you feel?" It seemed to really penetrate his fighter pilot brain as she continued, "Well, that's how I feel when you don't give me a simple card, or other small gift, except on holidays and my birthday. You only speak my love language about four times a year."

A couple of days later, Trent went on a TDY to Red Flag at Nellis AFB in Las Vegas, and came back with a large pair of bright pink dice for hanging on a rearview car mirror. Across the front of the dice, it said, "I'm lucky to have you. I love you."

It was a start. And though it didn't come naturally for Trent, his simple efforts helped Rachel feel loved.

If you discover your spouse's primary love language is receiving gifts, then perhaps you will understand that purchasing gifts for him or her is the best investment you can make. You are investing in your relationship and filling your spouse's emotional love tank, and with a full love tank, he or she will likely reciprocate emotional love to you in a language you will understand. When both persons' emotional needs are met, your marriage will take on a whole new dimension. Don't worry about your savings. You will always be a saver, but to invest in loving your spouse is to invest in blue-chip stocks.

## THE GIFT OF SELF

There is an intangible gift that sometimes speaks more loudly than a gift that can be held in one's hand. I call it the gift of self or the gift of presence. Being there when your spouse needs you speaks loudly to the one whose primary love language is receiving gifts. Jan once said to me, "My husband, Don, loves softball more than he loves me."

"Why do you say that?" I inquired.

"On the day our baby was born, he played softball. I was lying in the hospital all afternoon while he played softball," she said.

"Was he there when the baby was born?"

"Oh yes. He stayed long enough for the baby to be born, but ten minutes afterward, he left to play softball. I was devastated. It was such an important moment in our lives. I wanted us to share it together. I wanted him to be there with me. Don deserted me to play."

That husband may have sent her a dozen roses, but they would not have spoken as loudly as his presence in the hospital room beside her. I could tell Jan was deeply hurt by that experience. The "baby" was now fifteen years old, and she was talking about the event with all the emotion as though it had happened yesterday. I probed further. "Have you based your conclusion that Don loves softball more than he loves you on this one experience?"

"No," she said. "On the day of my mother's funeral, he also played softball."

"Did he go to the funeral?"

"Yes, he did. He went to the funeral, but as soon as it was over, he left to play softball. I couldn't believe it. My brothers and sisters came to the house with me, but my husband was playing softball."

Later, I asked Don about those two events. "I had done what I thought was important to her, but it wasn't enough," said Don. "She has never let me forget those two days. She says I love softball more than I love her. That's ridiculous."

He was a sincere husband who failed to understand the tremendous power of presence. His being there for his wife was more important than anything else in her mind. Physical presence in the time of crisis is the most powerful gift you can give if your spouse's primary love language is receiving gifts. Your body becomes the symbol of your love. Remove the symbol, and the sense of love evaporates. In counseling, Don and Jan worked through the hurts and misunderstandings of the past. Eventually, Jan was able to forgive him, and Don came to understand why his presence was so important to her.

If the physical presence of your spouse is important to you, I urge you to verbalize that to your spouse. Don't expect him to read your mind. If, on the other hand, your spouse says to you, "I really want you to be there with me tonight, tomorrow, this afternoon," take his request seriously. From your perspective, it may not be important; but if you are not responsive to that request, you may be communicating a message you do not intend.

When Claire's husband came home for R&R, he was a changed man. He had survived an attack of sixty mortars. Twelve of his comrades had not. But the last thing he wanted to do was talk about it. "Jake would sit in the living room by himself and wouldn't say anything, except to tell the kids to get away," said Claire. "I didn't know what to do. I just sat beside him on the couch and didn't say a word." Sometimes she put her hand on his knee or arm. One time she sat and held his hand for an hour. Sometimes he would squeeze her hand and cry. For eighteen days, she just sat with him as often as she could, never saying anything.

When the time came to bring him back to the airport, Jake gave her a big kiss and hug. "Sweetheart," he told her, "I've never felt closer to you than I have in the last few weeks." Claire was shocked. But from Jake's perspective, she had given him the gift of herself, with no strings attached. He would never forget those weeks of silent companionship.

## MIRACLE IN CHICAGO

Almost everything ever written on the subject of love indicates that at the heart of love is the spirit of giving. All five love languages challenge us to give to our spouse, but for some, receiving gifts, visible symbols of love, speaks the loudest. I heard the most graphic illustration of that truth in Chicago, where I met Doug and Kate.

They attended my marriage seminar and agreed to take me to O'Hare Airport after the seminar on Saturday afternoon. We had two or three hours before my flight, and they asked if I would like to stop at a restaurant. I was famished, so I readily assented.

Kate began talking almost immediately after we sat down. She said, "Dr. Chapman, God used you to perform a miracle in our marriage. Three years ago, we attended your marriage seminar here in Chicago for the first time. I was desperate," she said. "I was thinking seriously of leaving Doug and had told him so. Our marriage had been empty for a long time. I had given up. For years, I had complained to Doug that I needed his love, but he never responded. I grew to hate him.

"For years," she continued, "I tried to be a good wife. I did all the things I thought a good wife should do. I had sex with him because I knew that was important to him, but I felt no love coming from him. I felt like he stopped dating me after we got married and simply took me for granted. I felt used and unappreciated.

"When I talked to Doug about my feelings, he'd laugh at me and say we had as good a marriage as anybody else in the community. He didn't understand why I was so unhappy. He would remind me that the bills were paid, we had a nice house and a new car, I was free to work or not work outside the home, and I should be happy instead of complaining all the time. He didn't even try to understand my feelings. I felt totally rejected.

"Well, anyway," she said as she moved her tea and leaned forward, "we came to your seminar three years ago. I did not know what to expect, and frankly I didn't expect much. I didn't think anybody could change Doug. During and after the seminar, he didn't say too much.

"Then Monday afternoon, he came home from work and gave me a rose. 'Where did you get that?' I asked. 'I bought it from a street vendor,' he said. 'I thought you deserved a rose.' I started crying. 'Oh, Doug, that is so sweet of you.'

"On Tuesday he called me from the office to ask what I thought about his buying a pizza and bringing it home for dinner so I could enjoy a break from cooking. I told him I thought the idea was wonderful, and so he brought home a pizza and we had a fun time together. The children loved the pizza and thanked their father for bringing it. I actually gave him a hug and told him how much I enjoyed it.

"Dr. Chapman, you have to understand. This man had never given me a flower since the day we got married."

"When he came home on Wednesday, he brought each of the children a box of Cracker Jacks, and he had a small potted plant for me. He said he knew the rose would die, and he thought I might like something that would be around for a while. I was beginning to think I was hallucinating! I couldn't believe what Doug was doing or why he was doing it.

"Thursday night after dinner, he handed me a card with a message about his not always being able to express his love to me but hoping that the card would communicate how much he cared. 'Why don't we get a babysitter on Saturday night and the two of us go out for dinner?' he suggested. 'That would be wonderful,' I said. On Friday afternoon, he stopped by the cookie shop and bought each of us one of our favorite cookies. Again, he kept it as a surprise, telling us only that he had a treat for dessert.

"By Saturday night," she said, "I was in orbit. I had no idea what had come over Doug, or if it would last, but I was enjoying every minute of it. After our dinner at the restaurant, I said to him, 'Doug, you have to tell me what's happening. I don't understand.'"

She looked at me intently and said, "Dr. Chapman, you have to understand. This man had never given me a flower since the day we got married. He never gave me a card for any occasion. He always said, 'It's a waste of money; you look at the card and throw it away.' We'd been out to dinner one time in five years. He never bought the children anything and expected me to buy only the essentials. He had never brought a pizza home for dinner. He expected me to have dinner ready every night. I mean, this was a radical change in his behavior."

I turned to Doug and asked, "What did you say to her in the restaurant when she asked you what was going on?"

"I told her I had listened to your lecture on love languages at the seminar and I realized her love language was gifts. I also realized I had not given her a gift in years, maybe not since we had been married. I remembered when we were dating I used to bring her flowers and other small gifts, but after marriage I figured we couldn't afford that. I told her I had decided to try to get her a gift every day for one week and see if it made any difference in her. I had to admit I had seen a pretty big difference in her attitude during the week.

"I told her I realized what you said was really true, and learning the right love language was the key to helping another person feel loved. I said I was sorry I had been so dense for all those years and had failed to meet her need for love. I told her I really loved her and I appreciated all the things she did for me and the children. I told her with God's help, I was going to be a gift giver for the rest of my life.

"She said, 'But, Doug, you can't go on buying me gifts every day for the rest of your life. You can't afford that.' 'Well, maybe not every day,' I said, 'but at least once a week. That would be fifty-two more gifts per year than what you have received in the past five years.' I continued, 'And who said I was going to buy all of them? I might even make some of them, or I'll take Dr. Chapman's idea and pick a free flower from the front yard in the spring.'"

"I don't think he has missed a single week in three years," Kate said. "He is like a new man. You wouldn't believe how happy we have been. Our children call us lovebirds now. My tank is full and overflowing."

I turned to Doug and asked, "But what about you, Doug? Do you feel loved by Kate?"

"Oh, I've always felt loved by her, Dr. Chapman. She is the best housekeeper in the world. She is an excellent cook. She is wonderful about doing things for the children. I know she loves me." He smiled and said, "Now, you know what my love language is, don't you?"

I did, and I also knew why Kate had used the word *miracle*.

Gifts need not be expensive, nor must they be given weekly. But for some individuals, their worth has nothing to do with monetary value and everything to do with love.

## YOUR TURN

*Reflect on ways to give gifts even if finances are tight.*

## If your spouse's love language is Receiving Gifts:

1. Try a parade of gifts: Leave a box of candy for your spouse in the morning; have flowers delivered in the afternoon; give her a gift in

the evening. When your spouse asks, "What is going on?" you respond: "Just trying to fill your love tank!"

2. Let nature be your guide: The next time you take a walk through the neighborhood, keep your eyes open for a gift for your spouse. It may be a stone, a stick, or a feather. You may even attach special meaning to your natural gift. For example, a smooth stone may symbolize your marriage with many of the rough places now polished. A feather may symbolize how your spouse is the "wind beneath your wings."

3. Discover the value of "handmade originals." Make a gift for your spouse. This may require you to enroll in an art or crafts class: ceramics, silversmithing, painting, wood carving, etc. Your main purpose for enrolling is to make your spouse a gift. A handmade gift often becomes a family heirloom.

4. Give your spouse a gift every day for one week. It need not be a special week, just any week. I promise you it will become "The Week That Was!" If you are really energetic, you can make it "The Month That Was!" No—your spouse will not expect you to keep this up for a lifetime.

5. Keep a "Gift Idea Notebook." Every time you hear your spouse say, "I really like that," or "Oh, I would really like to have one of those!" write it down in your notebook. Listen carefully and you will get quite a list. This will serve as a guide when you get ready to select a gift. To prime the pump, you may look through a favorite online shopping site together.

6. Enlist a "personal shopper." If you really don't have a clue as to how to select a gift for your spouse, ask a friend or family member who knows your wife or husband well to help you. Most people enjoy making a friend happy by getting them a gift, especially if it's with your money.

7. Offer the gift of presence. Say to your spouse, "I want to offer the gift of my presence at any event or on any occasion you would like this month. You tell me when, and I will make every effort to be there." Get ready! Be positive! Who knows, you may enjoy the symphony or the hockey game.

8. Give your spouse a book and agree to read it yourself. Then offer to discuss together a chapter each week. Don't choose a book you want him or her to read. Choose a book on a topic in which you know your spouse has an interest: sex, football, needlework, money management, child rearing, religion, backpacking.

9. Give a lasting tribute. Give a gift to your spouse's church or favorite charity in honor of her birthday, your anniversary, or another occasion. Ask the charity to send a card informing your spouse of what you have done. The church or charity will be excited and so will your spouse.

10. Give a living gift. Purchase and plant a tree or flowering shrub in honor of your spouse. You may plant it in your own yard, where you can water and nurture it, or in a public park or forest where others can also enjoy it. You will get credit for this one year after

year. If it's an apple tree, you may live long enough to get an apple. One warning: Don't plant a crabapple tree!

## Decoding Deployments with Receiving Gifts

Speaking the gifts love language is still very possible during separations. It just requires a little more planning and creativity. Here are some ideas to get you started.

1. Send your service member care packages with favorite baked items and something he enjoys having, such as a special soap, food item, etc. Be sure to check regulations on what is allowed in packages first.
2. Create a special day honoring your service member. Have family and friends send cards, emails, care packages, which communicate their support of him.
3. Service member, bring home unique gifts for your spouse. Tell her when you've purchased it just so she knows you've been thinking of her.
4. For the service member's birthday, make and send a cake-sized brownie and place hard candy letters on it that say "Happy Birthday." Be sure to send candles, plates, napkins, and plastic forks so she can share it.
5. Service member, conspire with some mutual friends or church members to have care packages delivered to your spouse's doorstep on holidays or ordinary days.
6. Home front spouse, put together a themed care package with memories of one of your special days you shared together.

7. Create a coupon book for your spouse to redeem when you are together again.

8. During the Christmas holidays, send the service member a stocking filled with goodies. Make him his favorite Christmas cookies; send him a very small, decorated Christmas tree, or something that will have great meaning to him.

9. Celebrate Valentine's Day with special cards and gifts that are meaningful to you as a couple. Also remember birthdays, your anniversary, and Military Spouse Appreciation Day, which always falls on the Friday before Mother's Day.

10. Service member, order gifts online—books, flowers, coffee, restaurant gift cards—and have them sent directly to your spouse— no special occasion required.

# THE 5 LOVE LANGUAGES®

# CHAPTER 7

LOVE LANGUAGE #4

# Acts *of* Service

The ink was barely dry on their marriage certificate when Erin and Nathan moved to Fort Knox, Kentucky, for a nine-month assignment. Unaccustomed to military life, Erin was lonely in her new environment and not intellectually challenged the way she had been in the career she had just given up. And, she didn't know the first thing about how to be an Army wife. Nathan was busy in his new job and completely clueless as to why his bride was growing frustrated and resentful.

"He didn't realize I needed help to learn how to do the simplest things like getting an identification card so I could shop at the store, learning how to cash a check at the post bank, going to the doctor, or navigating the many offices and rules on post," said Erin. She felt thrown into a life where she knew very little, and Nathan was not speaking her love language to help her learn.

Erin's primary love language was what I call "acts of service." By acts of service, I mean doing things you know your spouse would like you to do. You seek to please her by serving her, to express your love for her by doing things for her. So it was with Doug, whom we met in the last chapter.

In a military marriage, "dependents" depend on the service member for help with certain tasks, such as getting an ID card, updating DEERS insurance accounts, securing passports, and finance or housing issues. All spouses need their service member to assist in these things (unless power of attorney allows otherwise), but spouses whose love language is acts of service will feel especially hurt, as Erin did, if their service members don't provide this help. Other day-to-day actions such as cooking a meal, setting a table, washing dishes, vacuuming, cleaning a commode, changing the baby's diaper, dusting the bookcase, keeping the car in operating condition, paying the bills, trimming the shrubs, walking the dog, changing the cat's litter box, and dealing with landlords and insurance companies are all acts of service. They require thought, planning, time, effort, and energy. If done with a positive spirit, they are indeed expressions of love.

Unfortunately, it never occurred to Nathan that Erin would need help with the basic aspects of adjusting to military life, and since she didn't feel loved and cared for by him, she withdrew physically from him. When he, in turn, seemed even less loving to her, she began to guess at possible reasons, ranging from regretting marrying her, to marrying her just to have a military spouse at his side in his career. "I learned and resented the old saying, 'If the Army would have wanted you to have a wife, they would have issued you one,'" Erin said.

A deployment, with its inherent communication breakdowns, only heightened tensions between them. "She seemed to hate military life," Nathan said. "I didn't know what to do, so I just worked harder to provide for us and avoided any arguments." In the meantime, on the home front, Erin volunteered at Army Community Service, where she was trained to teach new Army wives all about Army life.

Eventually, a chaplain gave Erin and Nathan tickets to attend a marriage seminar, and they discovered *The 5 Love Languages*. Finally, Erin and Nathan understood why they both felt frustrated. "We still loved each other very much, but being apart and living a demanding military life with many deployments made it far more difficult to speak the love languages of physical touch and acts of service," said Erin.

To ease some of the loneliness when he deployed, Nathan wrote a letter he would mail from the post the day he left. He also wrote a few letters to be opened in the days after he left. To Erin, taking the time to write letters and emails was an act of service.

——— ★ ★ ★ ———

"Can a couple make it in marriage if they disagree on everything?"

Nathan's primary love language was physical touch, but acts of service was his secondary. So Erin continued to perform acts of service at home with a greater love and understanding now that she had been trained to understand Army life by Army Community Service in the Army Family Team Building program. She became so passionate about helping other women avoid the pain she and Nathan had been through she became an award-winning volunteer, training other women, receiving the Helping Hands Award, and being inducted into the Order of Saint Joan D'Arc. Both Nathan and Erin have continued to read books about marriage and family, and live out a commitment of drawing closer in their marriage each day.

## CONVERSATION IN A MILL TOWN

I discovered the impact of "acts of service" in the little village of China Grove, North Carolina. I was standing under a chinaberry tree after church on Sunday when Mark and Mary approached me.

"I have a question," Mark said after introducing himself. "Can a couple make it in marriage if they disagree on everything?"

It was one of those theoretical questions I knew had a personal root, so I asked him a personal question. "How long have you been married?"

"Two years," he responded. "And we don't agree on anything."

"Give me some examples," I continued.

"Well, for one thing, Mary doesn't like me to go hunting. I work all week in the mill, and I like to go hunting on Saturdays—not every Saturday but when hunting season is in."

Mary had been silent until this point when she interjected. "When hunting season is out, he goes fishing, and besides, he doesn't hunt just on Saturdays. He takes off from work to go hunting."

"Once or twice a year I take off two or three days from work to go hunting in the mountains with some buddies. I don't think there is anything wrong with that."

"What else do you disagree on?" I asked.

"Well, she wants me to go to church all the time. I don't mind going on Sunday morning, but Sunday night I like to rest. It's all right if she wants to go, but I don't think I ought to have to go."

Again Mary spoke up. "You don't really want me to go either," she said. "You fuss every time I walk out the door."

I continued. "What other things do you disagree on?"

This time Mary answered. "He wants me to stay home all day and work in the house," she said. "He gets mad if I go see my mother or go shopping or something."

"I don't mind her going to see her mother," he said, "but when I come home, I like to see the house cleaned up. Some weeks, she doesn't make the bed up for three or four days, and half the time, she hasn't even started supper. I work hard, and I like to eat when I get home. Besides that, the house is a wreck," he continued. "The baby's things are all over the floor, the baby is dirty, and I don't like filth. She seems to be happy to live in a pigpen. We don't have very much, and we live in a small mill house, but at least it could be clean."

"What's wrong with his helping me around the house?" Mary asked. "He acts like a husband shouldn't do anything around the house. All he wants to do is work and hunt. He expects me to do everything."

Thinking I had better start looking for solutions rather than prying for more disagreements, I looked at Mark and asked, "Mark, when you were dating, before you got married, did you go hunting every Saturday?"

"Most Saturdays," he said, "but I always got home in time to go see her on Saturday night. Most of the time, I'd get home in time to wash my truck before I went to see her. I didn't like to go see her with a dirty truck."

"Mary, how old were you when you got married?" I asked.

"I was eighteen," she said. "We got married right after I finished high school. Mark graduated a year before me, and he was working."

"During your senior year in high school, how often did Mark come to see you?" I inquired.

"He came almost every night," she said. "In fact, he came in the afternoon and would often stay and have supper with my family. He would help me do my chores around the house and then we'd sit and talk until supper time."

"Mark, what did the two of you do after supper?" I asked.

Mark looked up with a sheepish smile and said, "Well, the regular dating stuff, you know."

"But if I had a school project," Mary said, "he'd help me with it. Sometimes we worked hours on school projects. I was in charge of the Christmas float for the senior class. He helped me for three weeks every afternoon. He was great."

I switched gears and focused on the third area of their disagreement. "Mark, when you were dating, did you go to church with Mary on Sunday nights?"

"Yes, I did," he said. "If I didn't go to church with her, I couldn't see her that night. Her father was strict that way."

I thought I was beginning to see some light, but I wasn't sure Mark and Mary were seeing it. I turned to Mary and asked, "When you were dating Mark, what convinced you he really loved you? What made him different from other guys you had dated?"

"It was the way he helped me with everything," she said. "He was so eager to help me. None of the other guys ever expressed any interest in those things, but it seemed natural for Mark. He even helped me wash dishes when he had supper at our house. He was the most wonderful person I had ever met, but after we got married that changed. He didn't help me at all."

Turning to Mark, I asked, "Why do you think you did all those things for and with her before you were married?"

"It just seemed natural for me," he said. "It's what I would want someone to do for me if she cared about me."

"And why do you think you stopped helping her after you got married?" I asked.

"Well, I guess I expected it to be like my family. Dad worked, and Mom took care of things at the house. I never saw my dad vacuum or wash the dishes or do anything around the house. Since Mom didn't work outside the house, she kept everything spotless, did all the cooking, washing, and ironing. And I guess I just thought that was the way it was supposed to be."

Hoping Mark was seeing what I was seeing, I asked, "Mark, a moment ago what did you hear Mary say when I asked her what really made her feel loved by you when you were dating?"

He responded, "Helping her with things and doing things with her."

"So, can you understand how she could feel unloved when you stopped helping her with things?" He was nodding yes. I continued. "It was a normal thing for you to follow the model of your mother and father in marriage. Almost all of us tend to do that, but your behavior toward Mary was a radical change from your courtship. The one thing that had assured her of your love disappeared."

Then I turned to Mary and asked, "What did you hear Mark say when I asked, 'Why did you do all of those things to help Mary when you were dating?'"

"He said it came naturally to him," she replied.

"That's right," I said, "and he also said that's what he would want some-

★ ★ ★

"Requests give direction to love, but demands stop the flow of love."

one to do for him if she loved him. He was doing those things for you and with you because in his mind that's the way anyone shows love. Once you were married and living in your own house, he had expectations of what you would do if you loved him. You would keep the house clean, you would cook, and so on. In brief, you would do things for him to express your love. When he did not see you doing those things, do you understand why he would feel unloved?" Mary was nodding now too. I continued, "My guess is that the reason you are both so unhappy in your marriage is that neither of you is showing your love by doing things for each other."

Mary said, "You're right, and the reason I stopped doing things for him is because I resented his demanding spirit. It was as if he were trying to make me be like his mother."

"You are right," I said, "and no one likes to be forced to do anything. In fact, love is always freely given. Love cannot be demanded. We can request things of each other, but we must never demand anything. Requests give direction to love, but demands stop the flow of love."

Mark broke in and said, "She's right. I was demanding and critical of her because I was disappointed in her as a wife. I know I said some cruel things, and I understand how she could be upset with me."

"I think things can be turned around rather easily at this juncture," I said. I pulled two note cards out of my pocket. "Let's try something. I want each of you to sit on the steps of the church and make a request list. Mark, I want you to list three or four things that if Mary chose to do them would make you feel loved when you walk into the house in the afternoon. If making the bed is important to you, then put it down. Mary, I want you to make a list of three or four things that you would really like to have Mark's help in doing, things that, if he chose to do them, would help you know he loved you." (I'm big on lists; they force us to think concretely.)

After five to six minutes, they handed me their lists. Mark's list read:

- Make up the beds every day.
- Have the baby's face washed when I get home.
- Put her shoes in the closet before I get home.

• Try to have supper at least started before I get home so we could eat within thirty to forty-five minutes after I get home.

I read the list out loud and said to Mark, "I'm understanding you to say that if Mary chooses to do these four things, you will view them as acts of love toward you."

"That's right," he said. "If she did those four things, it would go a long way in changing my attitude toward her."

Then I read Mary's list:

• I wish he would wash the car every week instead of expecting me to do it.
• I wish he would change the baby's diaper after he gets home in the afternoon, especially if I am working on supper.
• I wish he would vacuum the house for me once a week.
• I wish he would mow the grass every week in the summer and not let it get so tall that I am ashamed of our yard.

I said, "Mary, I am understanding you to say that if Mark chooses to do those four things, you would take his actions as genuine expressions of love toward you."

"I would," she said. "It would be wonderful if he would do those things for me."

"Does this list seem reasonable to you, Mark? Is it feasible for you to do these things?"

"Yes," he said.

"Mary, do the things on Mark's list seem reasonable and feasible to

★ ★ ★

What we do for each other before marriage is no indication of what we will do after marriage.

you? Could you do them if you chose to?"

"Yes," she said, "I can do those things. In the past, I have felt overwhelmed because no matter what I did, it was never enough."

I turned to Mark. "Mark, you understand what I am suggesting is a change from the model of marriage that your mother and father had."

"Oh, my father mowed the grass and washed the car."

"But he didn't change the diapers or vacuum the floor, right?"

"Right," he said.

"You don't have to do these, you understand? If you do them, however, it will be an act of love to Mary."

And to Mary I said, "You understand you don't have to do these things, but if you want to express love for Mark, here are four ways that will be meaningful to him. I want to suggest you try these for two months and see if they help. At the end of two months, you may want to add additional requests to your lists and share them with each other. I would not add more than one request per month, however."

"This really makes sense," Mary said. "I think you've helped us," Mark said. They took each other by the hand and walked toward their car. After years of research, I have realized what a unique situation Mark and Mary presented me. Seldom do I meet a couple who both have the same love language. For both Mark and Mary, "acts of service" was their primary love language. Hundreds of individuals can identify with either Mark or Mary and acknowledge that the primary way they feel loved is by acts of service on the part of their spouse. Putting away shoes, changing a baby's diaper, washing dishes or a car, vacuuming,

★ ★ ★

People tend to criticize their spouse most loudly in the area where they themselves have the deepest emotional need.

or mowing speaks volumes to the individual whose primary love language is acts of service.

You may be wondering, If Mark and Mary had the same primary love language, why were they having so much difficulty? The answer lies in the fact that they were speaking different dialects. They were doing things for each other but not the most important things. When they were forced to think concretely, they easily identified their specific dialects. For Mary it was washing the car, changing the baby's diaper, vacuuming the floor, and mowing the grass, whereas for Mark it was making up the bed, washing the baby's face, putting the shoes in the closet, and having supper under way when he got home from work.

When they started speaking the right dialects, their love tanks began to fill. Since acts of service was their primary love language, learning each other's specific dialect was relatively easy for them.

★ ★ ★

Love says, "I love you too much to let you treat me this way. It is not good for you or me."

Before we leave Mark and Mary, I would like to make three other observations. First, they illustrate clearly that what we do for each other before marriage is no indication of what we will do after marriage. Before marriage, we are carried along by the force of the "in love" obsession. After marriage, we revert to being the people we were before we "fell in love." Our actions are influenced by the model of our parents, our own personality, our perceptions of love, our emotions, needs, and desires. Only one thing is certain about our behavior: It will not be the same behavior we exhibited when we were caught up in being "in love."

That leads me to the second truth illustrated by Mark and Mary. Love is a choice and cannot be coerced. Mark and Mary were criticizing each other's behavior and getting nowhere. Once they decided to make requests of each other rather than demands, their marriage began to turn around. Criticism and demands tend to drive wedges. With enough criticism, you may get acquiescence from your spouse. He may do what you want, but probably it will not be an expression of love. You can give guidance to love by making requests: "I wish you would wash the car, change the baby's diaper, mow the grass," but you cannot create the will to love. Each of us must decide daily to love or not to love our spouses. If we choose to love, then expressing it in the way in which our spouse requests will make our love most effective emotionally.

There is a third truth, which only the mature lover will be able to hear. My spouse's criticisms about my behavior provide me with the clearest clue to her primary love language. People tend to criticize their spouse most loudly in the area where they themselves have the deepest emotional need. Their criticism is an ineffective way of pleading for love. If we understand that, it may help us process their criticism in a more productive manner. A wife may say to her husband after he gives her a criticism, "It sounds like that is extremely important to you. Could you explain why it is so crucial?" Criticism often needs clarification. Initiating such a conversation may eventually turn the criticism into a request rather than a demand. Mary's constant condemnation of Mark's hunting was not an expression of her hatred for the sport of hunting. She blamed hunting as the thing that kept him from washing the car, vacuuming the house, and mowing the grass. When he learned to meet her need for love by speaking her emotional love language, she became free to support him in his hunting.

## DOORMAT OR LOVER?

"I have served him for twenty years. I have waited on him hand

and foot. I have been his doormat while he ignored me, mistreated me, and humiliated me in front of my friends and family. I don't hate him. I wish him no ill, but I resent him, and I no longer wish to live with him." That wife has performed acts of service for twenty years, but they have not been expressions of love. They were done out of fear, guilt, and resentment.

A doormat is an inanimate object. You can wipe your feet on it, step on it, kick it around, or whatever you like. It has no will of its own. It can be your servant but not your lover. When we treat our spouses as objects, we preclude the possibility of love. Manipulation by guilt ("If you were a good spouse, you would do this for me") is not the language of love. Coercion by fear ("You will do this or you will be sorry") is alien to love. No person should ever be a doormat. We may allow ourselves to be used, but we are in fact creatures of emotion, thoughts, and desires. And we have the ability to make decisions and take action. Allowing oneself to be used or manipulated by another is not an act of love. It is, in fact, an act of treason. You are allowing him or her to develop inhumane habits. Love says, "I love you too much to let you treat me this way. It is not good for you or me."

Learning the love language of acts of service will require some of us to reexamine our stereotypes of the roles of husbands and wives. These are changing, but models from our past can linger. Mark was doing what most of us do naturally. He was following the role model of his father and mother, but he wasn't even doing that well. His father washed the car and mowed the grass. Mark did not, but that was the mental image he had of what a husband should do. He definitely did not picture himself vacuuming floors and changing the baby's diapers. To his credit, he was willing to break from his stereotype when he realized how important it was to Mary. That is necessary for all of us if our spouse's primary love language asks something of us that seems inappropriate to our role.

Some of us, however, resist doing things that do fall within our stereotypical role. When Scott and Laura married, they were both on their own career paths. Busy with her own job, Laura did not make cooking a priority. When Scott joined the military, they stayed with his parents while he completed Basic Training. "I watched how his mom cooked meals every night for her family," Laura remembered. "She worked full-time, just like I did, but she really served her family with those meals, and Scott responded so much to them. You could just tell his love tank was being filled by that act of service." Laura began to understand then that it wasn't about gender but about showing love in a way her husband appreciated.

Bryant learned the same lesson while trying to express and receive love with his deployed wife, Karen. At first, he showered her with romance—emails, love letters, and care packages—but his efforts were not rewarded. "For months, my frustration grew when words of my undying love were not reciprocated," Bryant said. "My frustration grew to anger, and before long resentment filled my heart."

But when Bryant read *The 5 Love Languages,* he understood he was not filling Karen's love tank, because her language was not words of affirmation or gifts but acts of service. "She didn't want to get those care packages on a weekly basis. She didn't want a couple letters each week or an email every night," he remembered. "She wanted me to do my job of taking care of the family while she was gone and nothing else really mattered. When I told her about what our kids and I were doing, I saw her love meter rise. By being more financially responsible, I was able to afford more outings with the kids. Pictures on Facebook showing us at the park or zoo or at an activity on our installation—that filled her tank and led her to meet my need through words of affirmation."

Due to the sociological changes of the past forty years, we no longer cling to certain notions of the male and female role in American society. Yet that does not mean all stereotypes have been eradicated. It means, rather, the *number* of stereotypes has multiplied. Before the days of widespread media influence, a person's idea of what a husband or wife should do and how he or she should relate was influenced primarily by one's own parents. With the pervasiveness of television, increased mobility, growing cultural diversity, and the proliferation of single-parent families, however, role models are often influenced by forces outside the home. Whatever your perceptions, chances are your spouse perceives marital roles somewhat differently than you do. A willingness to examine and change stereotypes is necessary in order to express love more effectively. Remember, there are no rewards for maintaining stereotypes, but there are tremendous benefits to meeting the emotional needs of your spouse.

Recently a wife said to me, "Dr. Chapman, I am going to send all of my friends to your seminar."

"And why would you do that?" I inquired.

"Because it has radically changed our marriage," she said. "Before the seminar, Bob never helped me with anything. We both started our careers right after college, but it was always my role to do everything at the house. It was as if it never crossed his mind to help me with anything. After the seminar, he started asking me, 'What can I do to help you this evening?' It was amazing. At first, I couldn't believe it was real, but it has persisted for three years now.

"I'll have to admit, there were some trying and humorous times in those early weeks because he didn't know how to do anything. The first time he did the laundry, he used undiluted bleach instead of regular detergent. Our blue towels came out with white polka dots. But he was loving me in my language, and my tank was filling up. Now he knows how to do everything around the house and is always helping me. We have much more time together because I don't have to work all the time. Believe me, I have learned his language, and I keep his tank full."

Is it really that simple?

Simple? Yes. Easy? No. Bob had to work hard at tearing down the stereotype with which he had lived for thirty-five years. It didn't come easily, but he would tell you that learning the primary love language of your spouse and choosing to speak it makes a tremendous difference in the emotional climate of a marriage.

## YOUR TURN

*Many acts of service will involve household chores, but not all. What are some non-chore ways of serving your mate?*

### If your spouse's love language is Acts of Service:

1. Make a list of all the requests your spouse has made of you over the past few weeks. Select one of these each week and do it as an expression of love.

2. Print note cards with the following:

   "Today I will show my love for you by . . ." Complete the sentence with one of the following: picking up the clutter, paying the bills, fixing something that's been broken a long time, weeding the garden. (Bonus points if it's a chore that's been put off.)

Give your spouse a love note accompanied by the act of service every three days for a month.

3. Ask your spouse to make a list of ten things he or she would like for you to do during the next month. Then ask your spouse to prioritize those by numbering them 1–10, with 1 being the most important and 10 being least important. Use this list to plan your strategy for a month of love. (Get ready to live with a happy spouse.)

4. While your spouse is away, get the children to help you with some act of service for him. When he walks in the door, join the children in shouting "Surprise! We love you!" Then share your act of service.

5. What one act of service has your spouse nagged about consistently? Why not decide to see the nag as a tag? Your spouse is tagging this as really important to him or her. If you choose to do it as an expression of love, it's worth more than a thousand roses.

6. If your requests to your mate come across as nags or putdowns, try writing them in words that would be less offensive to them. Share this revised wording with your spouse. For example, "The yard always looks so nice, and I really appreciate your work. I'd love to thank you in advance for mowing the lawn this week before Julie and Ben come over for dinner." Your husband might even respond: "Where's the lawn mower, I can't wait!" Try it and see.

7. Perform a major act of service like organizing the home office, and then post a sign that reads, "To (spouse's name) with love," and sign your name.

8. If you have more money than time, hire someone to do the acts of service you know your spouse would like for you to do, such as the yard work or a once-a-month deep cleaning of your home.

9. Ask your spouse to tell you the daily acts of service that would really speak love to him or her. Seek to work these into your daily schedule. "Little things" really do mean a lot.

## Decoding Deployments with Acts of Service

During deployments, service members should keep in mind that spouses on the home front are doing acts of service for them daily by managing the home front solo. Spouses on the home front would do well to remember their service members are also serving them (and others) in their line of duty. However, if this is your spouse's primary love language, going the extra mile to personalize the service will reap big rewards for your marriage.

1. To avoid needless frustration on the home front, be sure spouses have the necessary powers of attorney to manage affairs in the service member's absence. (Note that there are special powers of attorney in addition to general power of attorney.)

2. Service member, make sure your property or vehicles are in good working condition before you leave in order to make life easier while you are gone.

3. Home front spouse, connect with your in-laws and ask them to share recipes that were meaningful to them when your spouse was growing up. Make up a family recipe book and tell him about it.

4. Home front spouse, create a special place where your service member can relax after returning home. If he is a hunter, create a lodge atmosphere with fishing and hunting items, magazines, etc. If she loves reading, create a reading corner with a comfy chair, good light, and well-filled bookcase.

5. Set up a goal list for the house. Send before and after pictures to the service member so he or she can see your progress.

6. Service member, arrange for the lawn to be cared for, the bills to paid, etc., in your absence. Make sure the home front spouse has a list of numbers she can call when any need arises.

7. Service member, surprise the spouse at home with some maid service, or arrange child care through a mutual friend so the home front spouse can get out.

8. Home front spouse, instead of saving up a honey-do list for your service member, take care of things as they arise the best you can.

9. Service member, if your spouse is ill, email friends near your home and alert them. Ask your church to bring meals to your home or make a run to the pharmacy.

10. Service member, record yourself reading stories to your children. This will not only be a service to your spouse, who can sit back and let you "take over" during part of the bedtime routine, but it will keep you present in your children's daily lives.

# THE 5 LOVE LANGUAGES®

# CHAPTER 8

LOVE LANGUAGE #5

# Physical Touch

We have long known that physical touch is a way of communicating emotional love. Numerous research projects in the area of child development have made that conclusion: Babies who are held, hugged, and kissed develop a healthier emotional life than those who are left for long periods of time without physical contact.

Physical touch is also a powerful vehicle for communicating marital love. Holding hands, kissing, embracing, and sexual intercourse are all ways of communicating emotional love to one's spouse. For some individuals, physical touch is their primary love language. Without it, they feel unloved. With it, their emotional tank is filled, and they feel secure in the love of their spouse.

## THE POWER OF TOUCH

Of the five senses, touching, unlike the other four, is not limited to one localized area of the body. Tiny tactile receptors are located throughout the body. When those receptors are touched or pressed, nerves carry impulses to the brain. The brain interprets these impulses and we perceive the thing that touched us is warm or cold, hard or soft. It causes pain or pleasure. We may also interpret it as loving or hostile.

Some parts of the body are more sensitive than others. The difference is due to the fact that the tiny tactile receptors are not scattered evenly over the body but arranged in clusters. Thus, the tip of the tongue is highly sensitive to touch whereas the back of the shoulders is the least sensitive. The tips of the fingers and the tip of the nose are other extremely sensitive areas. Our purpose, however, is not to understand the neurological basis of the sense of touch but rather its psychological importance.

Physical touch can make or break a relationship. It can communicate hate or love. To the person whose primary love language is physical touch, the message will be far louder than the words "I hate you" or "I love you." A slap in the face is detrimental to any child, but it's devastating to a child whose primary love language is touch. A tender hug communicates love to any child, but it shouts love to the child whose primary love language is physical touch. The same is true of adults.

> ★ ★ ★
>
> Don't make the mistake of believing the touch that brings pleasure to you will also bring pleasure to her.

In marriage, the touch of love may take many forms. Since touch receptors are located throughout the body, lovingly touching your spouse almost anywhere can be an expression of love. That does not mean that all touches are created equal. Some will bring more pleasure to your spouse than others. Your best instructor is your spouse, of course. After all, she is the one you are seeking to love. She knows best what she perceives as a loving touch. Don't insist on touching her in your way and in your time. Learn to speak her love dialect. Your spouse may find some touches uncomfortable or irritating. To insist on continuing those touches is to communicate the opposite of love. It says you are not sensitive to her needs and you care little about her perceptions of what is pleasant. Don't make the mistake of believing the touch that brings pleasure to you will also bring pleasure to her.

Love touches may be explicit and demand your full attention such as in a back rub or sexual foreplay, culminating in intercourse. On the other hand, love touches may be implicit and require only a moment, such as putting your hand on his shoulder as you pour a cup of coffee or rubbing your body against him as you pass in the kitchen. Explicit love touches obviously take more time, not only in actual touching but in developing your understanding of how to communicate love to your spouse this way. If a back massage communicates love loudly to your spouse, then the time, money, and energy you spend in learning to be a good masseur or masseuse will be well invested. If sexual intercourse is your mate's primary dialect, reading about and discussing the art of sexual lovemaking will enhance your expression of love.

Implicit love touches require little time but much thought, especially if physical touch is not your primary love language and if you did not grow up in a "touching family." Sitting close to each other as you watch your favorite television program requires no additional time but may communicate your love loudly. Touching your spouse as you walk through the room where he is sitting takes only a moment. Touching each other when you leave the house and again when you return may involve only a brief kiss or hug but will speak volumes to your spouse.

Janie is one who did not grow up in a "touching" family. "So when

Ben returned from deployment, I felt like he was touching me all the time," she said. "It was a rough spot in our marriage. I was pregnant with our first child, we were in Alaska, and I just wanted him to stop touching me. It irritated me, and I thought it was piggish of him. I thought he was always wanting intimacy." She chalked it up to his selfishness, and considered herself in a one-sided marriage. Ben's response to her resistance was anger and defensiveness.

Then she read *The 5 Love Languages*. "Suddenly, I realized he was pouring love on me when he was touching me, because physical touch is his love language!" Janie said. "So I had a decision to make. Was I going to choose to love him the way he needed to be loved, or was I going to hold on to my personality and refuse to give him that?"

It still doesn't come naturally to Janie, but she deliberately speaks Ben's love language now. "If he comes into the kitchen, I will pat him first or touch his shoulder when I walk by," she said. "Immediately, when I made the change, the perceived clinginess subsided. The more I made an effort to meet his need, the less consuming it was to me."

Once you discover physical touch is the primary love language of your spouse, you are limited only by your imagination on ways to express love. Coming up with new ways and places to touch can be an exciting challenge. If you have not been an "under-the-table toucher," you might find it will add a spark to your dining out. If you are not accustomed to holding hands in public, you may find you can fill your spouse's emotional love tank as you stroll through the parking lot. If you don't normally kiss as soon as you get into the car together, you may find it will greatly enhance your travels. Hugging your spouse before

★ ★ ★

Clearly our bodies are for touching, but not for abuse.

she goes shopping may not only express love, it may bring her home sooner. Try new touches in new places and let your spouse give you feedback on whether he finds it pleasurable or not. Remember, he has the final word. You are learning to speak his language.

Just as important as learning physical touch is your spouse's love language may be the discovery that it is not. This was certainly the case for Vince and his wife, Audrey, who is active duty. Vince's primary love language is physical touch, but it barely registers on Audrey's list at all. "I often find myself becoming extremely jealous of the guys around her because, of course, in the military there are so many," said Vince. "In the past my heart soured at the thought of the lack of physical touch I received, but now I understand what fills my 'love tank' doesn't fill hers. So when she does go out of her way to offer me some sort of physical touch, it means so much more. Instead of being jealous and wondering how on earth she could not want my physical touch, thinking she must want someone else's, I now get it. I get that she isn't looking toward someone else for that physical touch, she just doesn't require it."

## THE BODY IS FOR TOUCHING

Whatever there is of me resides in my body. To touch my body is to touch me. To withdraw from my body is to distance yourself from me emotionally. In our society shaking hands is a way of communicating openness and social closeness to another individual. When on rare occasions one man refuses to shake hands with another, it communicates a message that things are not right in their relationship. All societies have some form of physical touching as a means of social greeting. The average American male may not feel comfortable with the European bear hug and kiss, but in Europe that serves the same function as our shaking hands.

There are appropriate and inappropriate ways to touch members of the opposite sex in every society. The recent attention to sexual harassment has highlighted the inappropriate ways. Within marriage, however, what is appropriate and inappropriate touching is determined by the couple themselves, within certain broad guidelines. Physical abuse is of course deemed inappropriate by society, and social organizations have been formed to help "the battered wife and the battered husband." Clearly our bodies are for touching, but not for abuse.

> ★ ★ ★
>
> If your spouse's primary love language is physical touch, nothing is more important than holding her as she cries.

This age is characterized as the age of sexual openness and freedom. With that freedom, we have demonstrated that the open marriage where both spouses are free to have sexual intimacies with other individuals is fanciful. Those who do not object on moral grounds eventually object on emotional grounds. Something about our need for intimacy and love does not allow us to give our spouse such freedom. The emotional pain is deep and intimacy evaporates when we are aware our spouse is involved with someone else sexually. Counselors' files are filled with records of husbands and wives who are trying to grapple with the emotional trauma of an unfaithful spouse. That trauma, however, is compounded for the individual whose primary love language is physical touch. That for which he longs so deeply—love expressed by physical touch—is now being given to another. His emotional love tank is not only empty; it has been riddled by an explosion. It will take massive repairs for those emotional needs to be met.

## CRISIS AND PHYSICAL TOUCH

Almost instinctively in a time of crisis, we hug one another. Why? Because physical touch is a powerful communicator of love. In a time of crisis, more than anything, we need to feel loved. We cannot always change events, but we can survive if we feel loved.

All marriages will experience crises. The death of parents is inevitable. Automobile accidents cripple and kill thousands each year. Disease is no respecter of persons. Disappointments are a part of life. The most important thing you can do for your mate in a time of crisis is to love him or her. If your spouse's primary love language is physical touch, nothing is more important than holding her as she cries. Your words may mean little, but your physical touch will communicate you care. Crises provide a unique opportunity for expressing love. Your tender touches will be remembered long after the crisis has passed. Your failure to touch may never be forgotten.

## "MARRIAGE IS NOT SUPPOSED TO BE THIS WAY"

Since my first visit to West Palm Beach, Florida, many years ago, I have always welcomed invitations to lead marriage seminars in that area. It was on one such occasion I met Pete and Patsy. They were not native to Florida (few are), but they had lived there for twenty years and called West Palm Beach home. My seminar was sponsored by a local church, and as we drove from the airport, the pastor informed me Pete and Patsy had requested I spend the night at their house. I tried to act excited, but knew from experience that such a request usually meant a late-night counseling session.

As the pastor and I entered the spacious, well-decorated, Spanish-style house, I was introduced to Patsy and to Charlie, the family cat. Pete came home shortly, and we had a delightful snack together and agreed we would have dinner after the seminar. Several hours later while sharing dinner, I kept waiting for the counseling session to begin. It never did. Instead, I found Pete and Patsy to be a healthy, happily married couple. For a counselor, that is an oddity. The next day, as we were driving to the airport, forty-five minutes away, Pete and Patsy shared their story. In the early years of their marriage, they had tremendous difficulties. They had grown up in the same community, attended the same church, and graduated from the same high school. Their parents had similar lifestyles and values. Pete and Patsy enjoyed many of the same things. They both liked tennis and boating, and they often talked about how many interests they held in common. They seemed to possess all the commonalities that are supposed to assure fewer conflicts in marriage.

They began dating in their senior year in high school. They attended separate colleges but saw each other frequently, and were married three weeks after he received his degree in business and she a degree in sociology. Two months later, they moved to Florida where Pete had been offered a good job. They were two thousand miles from their nearest relative. They could enjoy a "honeymoon" forever. The first three months were exciting—moving, finding a new apartment, enjoying life together.

They were about six months into the marriage when Patsy began to feel Pete withdrawing from her. He was working longer hours, and when he was at home, he spent considerable time with the computer. When she finally expressed her feelings that he was avoiding her, Pete told her he was not avoiding her but simply trying to stay on top of his job. He said she didn't understand the pressure he was under and how important it was that he do well in his first year on the job. Patsy wasn't pleased, but she decided to give him space.

Patsy began to develop friendships with other wives who lived in the apartment complex. Often when she knew Pete was going to work late, she would go shopping with one of her friends instead of going straight home after work. Sometimes she was not at home when Pete arrived. That annoyed him greatly, and he accused her of being thoughtless and irresponsible. Patsy retorted, "Who is irresponsible? You don't even call me and let me know when you will be home. How can I be here for you when I don't even know when you will be here? And when you are here, you spend all your time with that dumb computer. You don't need a wife; all you need is a computer!"

To which Pete loudly responded, "I do need a wife. Don't you understand? That's the whole point. I *do* need a wife."

But Patsy did not understand. She was extremely confused. In her search for answers, she went to the public library and checked out several books on marriage. "Marriage is not supposed to be this way," she reasoned. "I have to find an answer to our situation." When Pete went to the computer room, Patsy would pick up her book. In fact on many evenings, she read until midnight. On his way to bed, Pete would notice her and make sarcastic comments such as, "If you read that much in college, you would have made straight As." Patsy would respond, "I'm not in college. I'm in marriage, and right now, I'd be satisfied with a C." Pete went to bed without so much as a second glance.

At the end of the first year, Patsy was desperate. She had mentioned it before, but this time she calmly said to Pete, "I am going to find a marriage counselor. Do you want to go with me?"

But Pete answered, "I don't need a marriage counselor. I don't have time to go to a marriage counselor. I can't afford a marriage counselor."

★ ★ ★

"Once I waited for six weeks before she touched me at all."

"Then I'll go alone," said Patsy.

"Fine, you're the one who needs counseling anyway."

The conversation was over. Patsy felt totally alone, but the next week she made an appointment with a marriage counselor. After three sessions, the counselor called Pete and asked if he would be willing to come in to talk about his perspective on their marriage. Pete agreed, and the process of healing began. Six months later, they left the counselor's office with a new marriage.

I said to Pete and Patsy, "What did you learn in counseling that turned your marriage around?"

"In essence, Dr. Chapman," Pete said, "we learned to speak each other's love language. The counselor did not use that term, but as you gave the lecture today, the lights came on. My mind raced back to our counseling experience, and I realized that's exactly what happened to us. We finally learned to speak each other's love language."

"So what is your love language, Pete?" I asked.

"Physical touch," he said without hesitation.

★ ★ ★

"I would go weeks without touching him. It didn't cross my mind."

"Physical touch for sure," said Patsy.

"And yours, Patsy?"

"Quality time, Dr. Chapman. That's what I was crying for in those days while he was spending all his time with his job and his computer."

"How did you learn physical touch was Pete's love language?"

"It took a while," Patsy said. "Little by little, it began to come out in the counseling. At first, I don't think Pete even realized it."

"She's right," Pete said. "I was so insecure in my own sense of self-worth that it took forever for me to be willing to identify and acknowledge that her lack of touch had caused me to withdraw. I never told her I wanted to be touched, although I was crying inside for her to reach out and touch me. In our dating relationship, I had always taken the initiative in hugging, kissing, and holding hands, but she had always been responsive. I felt she loved me, but after we got married, there were times I reached out to her physically and she was not responsive. Maybe with her new job responsibilities, she was too tired. I don't know, but I took it personally. I felt she didn't find me attractive. Then I decided I would not take the initiative because I didn't want to be rejected. So I waited to see how long it would be before she'd initiate a kiss or a touch or sexual intercourse. Once I waited for six weeks before she touched me at all. I found it unbearable. My withdrawal was to stay away from the pain I felt when I was with her. I felt rejected, unwanted, and unloved."

Then Patsy said, "I had no idea that was what he was feeling. I knew he was not reaching out to me. We were not kissing and hugging as we had done earlier, but I just assumed that since we were married, that was not as important to him now. I knew he was under pressure with his job. I had no idea he wanted me to take the initiative.

"I would go weeks without touching him. It didn't cross my mind. I was preparing meals, keeping the house clean, doing the laundry, and trying to stay out of his way. I honestly didn't know what else I could be doing. I could not understand his withdrawal or his lack of attention to me. It's not that I dislike touching; it just was never that important to me. Spending time with me is what made me feel loved and appreciated, giving me attention. It really didn't matter whether we hugged or kissed. As long as he gave me his attention, I felt loved.

"It took us a long time to discover the root of the problem, but once we discovered we were not meeting each other's emotional need for love, we began to turn things around. Once I began to take the initiative in giving him physical touch, it's amazing what happened. His personality, his spirit changed drastically. I had a new husband. Once he became convinced I really did love him, then he began to become more responsive to my needs."

Pete is only one of many individuals for whom physical touch is the primary love language. Emotionally, they yearn for their spouse to reach out and touch them physically. Running the hand through the hair, giving a back rub, holding hands, embracing, sexual intercourse—all of those and other "love touches" are the emotional lifeline of the person for whom physical touch is the primary love language.

## YOUR TURN

*Recall some nonsexual "touching times" that enhanced intimacy between the two of you. What made these times special?*

### *If your spouse's love language is Physical Touch:*

1. As you walk from the car to go shopping, reach out and hold your spouse's hand.

2. While eating together, let your knee or foot drift over and touch your spouse.

3. Walk up to your spouse and say, "Have I told you lately that I love you?" Take her in your arms and hug her while you rub her back and continue. "You are the greatest!" (Resist the temptation to rush to the bedroom.) Untangle yourself and move on to the next thing.

4. While your spouse is seated, walk up behind her and give her a shoulder massage.

5. When you sit together in church, when the minister calls for prayer, reach over and hold your spouse's hand.

6. Initiate sex by giving your spouse a foot massage. Continue to other parts of the body as long as it brings pleasure to your spouse.

7. When family or friends are visiting, touch your spouse in their presence. A hug, running your hand along his or her arm, putting your arm around him as you stand talking, or simply placing your hand on her shoulder can earn double emotional points. It says, "Even with all these people in our house, I still see you."

8. When your spouse arrives at home, meet him or her one step earlier than usual and give your mate a big welcome home. The point is to vary the routine and enhance even a small "touching experience."

---

## *Decoding Deployments with Physical Touch*

Spouses whose primary love language is physical touch have a difficult time feeling loved during deployments. As with the quality time love language, you may want to increase your efforts on your spouse's secondary love language to help compensate for the deficit he or she feels while apart. Also try the following suggestions.

1. When talking or emailing, say things like, "I wish I could give you a big hug right now," or, "If I were with you, I'd give you a back massage to ease some of the tension away."

2. Send pictures of yourself to your spouse at various times while apart. Being able to hold a photo of you becomes very important when holding you in person is impossible.

3. Next time you have your hair cut, save a lock of it and send it to your spouse.

4. Spray some perfume or cologne you normally wear on a card or piece of fabric and send it to your spouse. Wives, be sure to seal your card with a kiss (wear some lipstick when you do this).

5. Trace your hand on paper and mail it to your spouse. He or she can high-five it or lay a hand on it to help feel connected to you.

6. Service members, arrange for a professional massage for your spouse at home. When you're not around, your spouse may go for weeks or months without human touch.

7. Send handwritten letters. Unlike emails, these are tangible pieces of your love that your spouse can touch.

8. Wives at home, if physical touch is your love language, try wearing a special clothing item of your husband's with his cologne placed on it. Marlene said, "I have developed a tradition of wearing my husband's denim shirt or robe around the house while my husband is away. It feels like he is hugging me when I wear it."

9. More tips for the spouse at home with a physical touch love language: Use a heated blanket on the empty side of the bed, so the bed won't feel cold. Sleep with pillows next to you so you don't get used to having the bed all to yourself. Spray a small amount of your spouse's cologne or perfume on the pillowcase or a sachet you place inside it. Don't replace the empty spot with a child or your child will get used to sleeping there. When your spouse returns home, your child might become fearful or resent him or her for taking his or her space in your bed.

# THE 5 LOVE LANGUAGES®

# CHAPTER 9

# Love Language Scramblers

Some aspects of military life make it especially challenging to interpret and express love. These are love language scramblers, the experiences that can cause mixed signals and tangled lines of communication. Let's look at just a few of these together.

## TACTICS TRAINING

Service members are trained to operate in a hierarchy, to take orders and give them, to complete missions. Emotions are irrelevant, and order and obedience are critical for the military to function. But in marriage, the military style of communication can drown out any love language.

"My instructions during my time overseas were simple: do your job, and do it now," said Vernon. "I became good at it, and enjoyed the time, because my schedule was often predictable, and my training sufficient to handle most pressures I faced."

But when he came home and tried the same approach to meet his wife, Jackie's, love language, his mission failed. "At work, when given an order or task, the expectation is that it gets done with little to no delay; this laser focus is necessary in meeting mission assignments. I call this 'running sprints' in relationship building. It took me a long time to understand that relationship building at home is more of a marathon.

——— ★ ★ ★ ———

Love begins with an attitude, moves to actions, and often stimulates positive emotions.

I needed to slow down on my approach and understand that once a 'task' has been completed at home, there are many other skills that need to be developed, like becoming an empathetic listener, and speaking my wife and children's love language. This for me was a new type of training that would be a lifetime of practice, making mistakes, learning from them, and trying again."

Military training, to obey orders without reference to your emotions, can be extremely helpful in speaking your spouse's love language. You don't need warm feelings to do acts of service or words of affirmation. Love begins with an attitude, moves to actions, and often stimulates positive emotions.

## WHEN DUTY CALLS

Separations can mask a person's love language simply because of the limits they impose on time spent together. Vernon and Jackie spent most of their engagement on two different continents, and, due to a deployment, didn't live together until six months into their marriage. During that time, neither realized their primary love languages were as far apart as their zip codes.

After redeployment, however, it became painfully clear.

"One day Vernon surprised me by coming home from work for lunch," said Jackie. "When I heard the door, I ran to hide in the closet so I could surprise and seduce him. When I jumped out, I was the one in for a surprise. He felt so unloved by the dirty dishes and clutter he saw that he was not 'in the mood.' Vernon turned around and left, confused, angry, and discouraged." Finally, it clicked for Jackie. "Vernon's love language is acts of service, and mine is quality time."

Five children later, the chaos in the household bothered Vernon much more than it bothered Jackie. Though Vernon helped with household duties as much as he could, the chaos that remained left him feeling tired, frustrated, and unwilling to give his wife the time and words she craved. "Sad to say, it was often a relief to go on multiple-day field exercises and deployments to get away from the pressures of daily trying to please my wife," Vernon said.

It's easy to see separations as time off from loving one's spouse the way they want to be loved, but the need for love does not go away. The key is learning to speak each other's language when you are together and then learning to speak it when apart.

Though it has taken years to learn to read him better, Jackie now knows how to speak Vernon's language. "Recently, I stayed up all night to clean the house to demonstrate my love for him, and it changed the entire climate of our home in minutes after he saw what had been done."

Dual military couples have the added challenge of juggling two sets of orders. When Carmen and Garrett were dating, both were active duty with overlapping deployments. Sometimes, they were literally two ships passing in the night, inbound and outbound in the Boston Harbor ship channel. "Those were tough days," said Carmen. "We weren't together long enough to get used to being together, and there was always another deployment hanging over our heads. We fought a lot. Not quite constantly, but we weren't married yet. I often wondered if we'd make it that far."

Eventually they discovered *The 5 Love Languages* and realized that in the limited time they did have together, their love was lost in translation. With short intervals together, each of them standing duty one or more days per week, and under pressure to earn qualifications, there was very little time to fill each other's "love tank." When they were together, they spoke the love language that came most naturally—their own. "But he didn't want a new shirt or something useful for his kitchen," said Carmen. "He wanted me to hold his hand and affirm him. And I would have been happy to know he was thinking of me while he was bouncing around those Caribbean islands, even if all he brought me was a shell necklace. Once we knew how the other 'heard' love, we could be more deliberate in how we spoke love to one another." Carmen and Garrett have now been married for fifteen years.

Learning to speak each other's love language can keep love alive even when we are worlds apart physically.

## REINTEGRATION

If a piano player stops playing music for an extended period of time, chances are, when he finally does sit at the piano again, his music may be a bit rusty. His mind will tell his fingers what to do, but they've been out of practice and are bound to hit a few wrong notes. He may need to drill a passage a few times before it feels natural and sounds beautiful again.

In the same way, deployments interrupt a marriage's natural rhythm. When you and your spouse are together again, you may find some skills need to be relearned.

For months, Meredith and Austin looked forward to his homecoming from his first deployment. But the extended honeymoon feeling they had expected did not match reality. "Reintegration was tough," said Austin. "I remember walking in the door and being overwhelmed by all the people who wanted my one-on-one attention; three little ones at my ankles, and my beautiful wife face-to-face. Being apart for so long, and not having so much attention directed at me, I struggled to give her the attention I wanted to give her."

A given amount of time spent together after deployment may not be enough for the spouse who craves quality time, and a suffocating amount for someone else. Patience and grace are key ingredients for easing the transition. "We had to relearn how to speak our love languages in the flesh," said Meredith. "The quality time and physical touch switches we had turned off were a bit harder to just turn back on. But after lots of tears and communication, we arrived at an even better place than before."

If you've had to put your love language on hold for an extended time, you may feel anxious for your empty love tank to be filled, while at the same time, your spouse may also have a depleted love tank and their energy level may be low. The greater the need and expectation, the greater the potential for disappointments, hurts, and offense during reintegration. I encourage couples to give each other permission to ease into things and be as patient with each other as possible during this time. You may both hit a few wrong notes as you switch from playing a solo to playing a duet, but keep at it! Harmony takes practice.

Communicating love for each other during reintegration is absolutely critical. During times apart, both spouses change as individuals. Now it's time to grow as a couple again.

People whose love languages are words of affirmation and receiving gifts tend to experience more conflict during reintegration, likely because these two languages were well-developed during separation through emails, letters, phone calls, and care packages or gifts. During reintegration, these expressions of love usually drop off—but they don't have to. If you continue to send emails and write letters to each other, or share small gifts, if that's your spouse's love language, both of you will benefit. Those who have gone to support groups during deployment will find continued encouragement from the group valuable during reintegration, as well.

If your spouse's love language is acts of service, use discernment during reintegration as to how to express this. Organizing the service member's gear may not be welcome. Taking over the family schedule may cause resentment to the spouse at home if he or she feels it's an indication of disapproval. I suggest you ask, "Would it be helpful to you if I . . . ?" Spend your energy in something that is meaningful to your spouse.

> ★ ★ ★
>
> The absence of romantic feelings does not mean your love has died or your marriage is doomed.

Janet, an active duty soldier herself, shared: "The hardest thing was my husband and I realizing that if I had to, I could 'do it' on my own. I can work, go to school, raise four children, and take care of a house without him. That's not how we *want* to live, but realizing that someone you love doesn't need you is a hard pill to swallow. We struggled adjusting because my husband felt he missed so much, he wanted to take over everything, which of course made me upset because he was uprooting the schedule that gave me and the children stability and a means of emotional survival. We had to sit down at the drawing board and come up with a new routine that was comfortable for all of us."

## COMBAT REDEPLOYMENT

When Ted was deployed to the Middle East, he found that, while driving, his mind drifted to missing his wife and children. "Then I thought, that's going to distract me," he recalled. "I might get ambushed. It might get me killed." So he pushed the memories away and used emotional compartmentalization as a survival technique.

Nine months later, he expected a blissful reunion with his wife. "But when I looked at her, I just felt numb. I didn't feel any love. I had stuffed those emotions so deep inside myself, I did not permit myself to bring them back up. It was an unconscious process."

Three months later, Ted once again felt the love he had for his wife. For others, it may take longer for those feelings to return. The absence of romantic feelings does not mean your love has died or your marriage is doomed. Regardless of what one feels, speaking the right love language can and should still be done. (More on this in chapter 11.)

Emotional withdrawal is common for both spouses. The person who once loved quality conversation and focused attention may now have a difficult time sharing his or her heart. For the service member, part of this is an effort to protect his or her family from the experiences and memories. Bekah felt emotionally single while her husband was engulfed in his own battle with PTSD. "It's simply self-protection," she said. "Learning to live in a two-way marriage again has challenged me in so many ways, even now, seven years after he returned from Iraq. Still today I went back to what I learned about love languages when we 'missed' each other again during 'date day' (we no longer do date nights due to crowds). He still has a wounded heart that needs affirmation more than ever. We are growing, learning to communicate again, and, as always, it's a process. We are imperfect in so many ways, but our heart is for the other to know they are loved."

When Hunter's post-traumatic stress was at its worst, physical touch became the most important thing to him. "It was his only connection to someone, and the only one he would connect with for physical touch was me," said his wife, Kara. Hunter experienced other bodily injuries, as well, which forced him to scale back on the acts of service he could do for Kara. With her primary love language not being spoken, Kara grew resentful and burned out. She learned to receive love from Hunter in different ways, but also looked for resources for caregivers for much-needed support.

Gail's husband, whose love language had been acts of service, needed something else upon redeployment. "After his deployment he had nightmares. We live on a large training base in Europe, so we hear a lot of loud 'booms' throughout the night and those really got to him for a while. I had to wake him up a lot. I could tell he was embarrassed about it, so I had to repeatedly tell him it didn't make him weak. I had to tell him all the time how amazing he is for going through what he did. At that time, he needed words of affirmation from me more than anything."

Rick saw three of his team killed on the same day. At the time of the event, Rick gutted through his pain and continued his job. However, two months later he started having flashbacks and nightmares. When he arrived home from deployment, his wife, Debbie, knew he was not functioning normally. She insisted he see a medical doctor. He was diagnosed with PTSD. Medication and counseling was the preferred treatment. Six months later, Rick was greatly improved.

He said, "These were the hardest months of my life. I'm sure I confused Debbie. My moods changed so quickly. One day I wanted her to hug me, but the next day I pushed her away. (My love language is physical touch.) I'm just glad she did not give up but kept speaking my love language. I love her more for putting up with my erratic behavior."

When PTSD or traumatic brain injury is present, the love languages may shift or require adaptations, such as Bekah and her husband avoiding crowds when they spend quality time together. PTSD is a topic worthy of more space than we have here in this chapter. There are many resources for veterans and spouses dealing with combat trauma. I recommend my favorites at 5lovelanguages.com/militaryedition.

# THE 5 LOVE LANGUAGES®

# CHAPTER 10

# Discovering Your Primary Love Language

D iscovering the primary love language of your spouse is essential if you are to keep their emotional love tank full. But first, let's make sure you know your own love language. Having heard the five emotional love languages,

> Words of Affirmation
> Quality Time
> Receiving Gifts
> Acts of Service
> Physical Touch,

some individuals will know instantaneously their own primary love language and that of their spouse. For others, it will not be that easy. Some are like Marcus, whom I met at Ft. Bragg. After hearing the five emotional love languages, he said to me, "I don't know. Two of those are just about equal for me."

"Which two?" I inquired.

"'Physical Touch' and 'Words of Affirmation,'" he responded.

"By 'Physical Touch,' what do you mean?"

"Well, mainly sex," Marcus replied.

I probed a little further, asking, "Do you enjoy your wife running her hands through your hair, or giving you a back rub, or holding hands, or kissing and hugging you at times when you are not having sexual intercourse?"

"Those things are fine," said Marcus. "I'm not going to turn them down, but the main thing is sexual intercourse. That's when I know that she really loves me."

Leaving the subject of physical touch for a moment, I turned to affirming words and asked, "When you say that 'Words of Affirmation' are also important, what kinds of statements do you find most helpful?"

"Almost anything if it's positive," Marcus replied. "When she tells me how good I look, how smart I am, what a hard worker I am, when she expresses appreciation for the things I do around the house, when she makes positive comments about my taking time with the children, when she tells me she loves me—all of those things really mean a lot to me."

"Let me ask you this. If you were having quality sexual intercourse as often as you desire, but Alicia was giving you negative words, making critical remarks, sometimes putting you down in front of others, do you think you would feel loved by her?"

"I don't think so," he replied. "I would feel betrayed and deeply hurt. I think I would be depressed."

"Marcus," I said, "I think we have just discovered your primary love language is 'Words of Affirmation.' Sexual intercourse is extremely important to you and to your sense of intimacy with Alicia, but her words of affirmation are more important to you emotionally. If she were verbally critical of you all the time and put you down in front of other people, the time may come when you would no longer desire to have sexual intercourse with her because she would be a source of deep pain to you."

Marcus had made the mistake common to many men: assuming "Physical Touch" is their primary love language because they desire sexual intercourse so intensely. For the male, sexual desire is physically based. That is, the desire for sexual intercourse is stimulated by the buildup of sperm cells and seminal fluid in the seminal vesicles. When the seminal vesicles are full, there is a physical push for release. Thus, the male's desire for sexual intercourse has a physical root.

For the female, sexual desire is far more influenced by her emotions. If she feels loved and admired and appreciated by her husband, then she has a desire to be physically intimate with him. But without the emotional closeness, she may have little physical desire. Her biological sexual drive is closely tied to her emotional need for love.

★ ★ ★

What makes you feel most loved by your spouse? What do you desire above all else?

Because the male is physically pushed to have sexual release on a somewhat regular basis, he may automatically assume that is his primary love language. But if he does not enjoy physical touch at other times and in nonsexual ways, it may not be his love language at all. Sexual desire is quite different from his emotional need to feel loved. That doesn't mean sexual intercourse is unimportant to him—it's extremely important—but sexual intercourse alone will not meet his need to feel loved. His wife must speak his primary emotional love language as well.

When, in fact, his wife speaks his primary love language and his emotional love tank is full, and he speaks her primary love language and her emotional tank is full, the sexual aspect of their relationship will take care of itself. Most sexual problems in marriage have little to do with physical technique but everything to do with meeting emotional needs.

After further conversation and reflection, Marcus said, "You know, I think you're right. 'Words of Affirmation' is definitely my primary love language. When she has been cutting and critical of me verbally, I tend to withdraw from her sexually and fantasize about other women. But when she tells me how much she appreciates me and admires me, my natural sexual desires are turned toward her." Marcus had made a significant discovery in our brief conversation.

## HOW DO YOU KNOW?

What is your primary love language? What makes you feel most loved by your spouse? What do you desire above all else? If the answer to those questions does not leap to your mind immediately, perhaps it will help to look at the negative use of love languages. What does your spouse do or say or fail to do or say that hurts you deeply? If, for example, your deepest pain is the critical, judgmental words of your spouse, then perhaps your love language is "Words of Affirmation." If your primary love language is used negatively by your spouse—that is, he does the opposite—it will hurt you more deeply than it would hurt someone else because not only is he neglecting to speak your primary love language, he is actually using that language as a knife to your heart.

I remember Mary in Ohio, who said, "Dr. Chapman, what hurts me most is that Ron never lifts a hand to help me around the house. He watches television while I do all the work. I don't understand how he could do that if he really loved me." Mary's deepest hurt, mainly that Ron did not help her do things around the house, was the clue to her primary love language—"Acts of Service." If it grieves you deeply that your spouse seldom gives you a gift for any occasion, then perhaps your primary love language is "Receiving Gifts." If your deepest hurt is that your spouse seldom gives you quality time, then that is your primary love language.

Another approach to discovering your primary love language is to look back over your marriage and ask, "What have I most often requested of my spouse?" Whatever you have most requested is probably in keeping with your primary love language. Those requests have probably been interpreted by your spouse as nagging. They have been, in fact, your efforts to secure emotional love from your spouse.

You can also examine what you do or say to express love to your spouse. Chances are what you are doing for her is what you wish she would do for you. If you are constantly doing "Acts of Service" for your spouse, perhaps (although not always) that is your love language. If "Words of Affirmation" speak love to you, chances are you will use them in speaking love to your spouse. Thus, you may discover your own language by asking, "How do I consciously express my love to my spouse?"

But remember, that approach is only a possible clue to your love language; it's not an absolute indicator. For example, the husband who learned from his father to express love to his wife by giving her nice gifts expresses his love to his wife by doing what his father did, yet "Receiving Gifts" is not his primary love language. He is simply doing what he was trained to do by his father.

I have suggested three ways to discover your own primary love language:

1. What does your spouse do or fail to do that hurts you most deeply? The opposite of what hurts you most is probably your love language.
2. What have you most often requested of your spouse? The thing you have most often requested is likely the thing that would make you feel most loved.
3. In what way do you regularly express love to your spouse? Your method of expressing love may be an indication that that would also make you feel loved.

Using those three approaches will probably enable you to determine your primary love language. If two languages seem to be equal for you, that is, both speak loudly to you, then perhaps you are bilingual. If so, you make it easier on your spouse. Now he or she has two choices, either of which will strongly communicate love to you.

★ ★ ★

Your picture of a perfect mate should give you some idea of your primary love language.

You may also wish to take the 5 Love Languages Profile found on pages 203–13. Discuss the results with your spouse.

Two kinds of people may have difficulty discovering their primary love language. The first is the individual whose emotional love tank has been full for a long time. Her spouse has expressed love in many ways, and she is not certain which of those ways makes her feel most loved. She simply knows she is loved. The second is the individual whose love tank has been empty for so long he doesn't remember what makes him feel loved. In either case, go back to the experience of falling in love and ask yourself, "What did I like about my spouse in those days? What did he do or say that made me desire to be with him?" If you can conjure up those memories, it will give you some idea of your primary love language. Another approach would be to ask yourself, "What would be an ideal spouse to me? If I could have the perfect mate, what would she be like?" Your picture of a perfect mate should give you some idea of your primary love language.

Having said all of that, let me suggest you spend some time writing down what you think is your primary love language. Then list the other four in order of importance. Also write down what you think is the primary love language of your spouse. You may also list the other four in order of importance if you wish. Sit down with your spouse and discuss what you guessed to be his/her primary love language. Then tell each other what you consider to be your own primary love language.

Once you have shared that information, I suggest you play the following game three times a week for three weeks. The game is called "Tank Check," and it's played like this. When you come home, one of you says to the other, "On a scale of 0 to 10, how is your love tank tonight?" Zero means empty, and 10 means "I am full of love and can't handle any more." You give a reading on your emotional love tank—10, 9, 8, 7, 6, 5, 4, 3, 2, 1, or 0, indicating how full it is. Your spouse says, "What could I do to help fill it?"

Then you make a suggestion—something you would like your spouse to do or say that evening. To the best of his ability, he will respond to your request. Then you repeat the process in the reverse order so both of you have the opportunity to do a reading on your love tank and to make a suggestion toward filling it. If you play the game for three weeks, you will be hooked on it, and it can be a playful way of stimulating love expressions in your marriage.

One military husband said to me, "I don't like that love tank game. I played it with my wife. I came home and said to her, 'On a scale of zero to ten, how's your love tank tonight?' She said, 'About seven.' I asked, 'What could I do to help fill it?' She said, 'The greatest thing you could do for me tonight is to do the laundry.' I said, 'Love and laundry? I don't get it.'"

⎯⎯ ★ ★ ★ ⎯⎯

"I'll wash the clothes every night if it makes her feel that good."

I said, "That's the problem. Perhaps you don't understand your wife's love language. What's your primary love language?"

Without hesitation he said, "Physical touch, and especially the sexual part of the marriage."

"Listen to me carefully," I said. "The love you feel when your wife expresses love by physical touch is the same love your wife feels when you do the laundry."

"Bring on the laundry," he shouted. "I'll wash the clothes every night if it makes her feel that good."

Incidentally, if you have still not discovered your primary love language, keep records on the tank check game. When your spouse says, "What could I do to help fill your tank?" your suggestions will likely cluster around your primary love language. You may request things from all five love languages, but you will have more requests centering on your primary love language.

Perhaps some of you are saying in your minds what one military couple said to me. "Dr. Chapman, all that sounds fine and wonderful, but what if the love language of your spouse is something that just doesn't come naturally for you?"

I'll discuss my answer in chapter 11.

## YOUR TURN

*Do you think by now you have a good sense of what your spouse's love language is? How about them for you? What more could you do to explore this? If your love tank is completely empty or very full, whether you know your love language or not, play the "Tank Check" game over the next month. Ask for a reading from 0 to 10 three evenings a week, and then take the suggestions of your spouse to raise that number for him/her. If your spouse is at a "ten" consistently you can pat yourself on the back—but don't stop loving.*

# THE 5 LOVE LANGUAGES®

# CHAPTER 11

# Love *Is* a Choice

How can we speak each other's love language when we are full of hurt, anger, and resentment over past failures? The answer to that question lies in the essential nature of our humanity. We are creatures of choice. That means that we have the capacity to make poor choices, which all of us have done. We have spoken critical words, and we have done hurtful things. We are not proud of those choices, although they may have seemed justified at the moment. Poor choices in the past don't mean we must make them in the future. Instead we can say, "I'm sorry. I know I have hurt you, but I would like to make the future different. I would like to love you in your language. I would like to meet your needs." I have seen marriages rescued from the brink of divorce when couples make the choice to love.

Love doesn't erase the past, but it makes the future different. When we choose active expressions of love in the primary love language of our spouse, we create an emotional climate where we can deal with our past conflicts and failures.

## "I JUST DON'T LOVE HER ANYMORE"

Brent was in my office, stone-faced and seemingly unfeeling. He had come not by his own initiative but at my request. A week earlier his wife, Becky, had been sitting in the same chair, weeping uncontrollably. Between her outbursts of tears, she managed to verbalize that Brent had told her he no longer loved her and he was leaving. She was devastated.

When she regained her composure, she said, "We have both worked so hard the last two or three years. I knew we were not spending as much time together as we used to, but I thought we were working for a common goal. I cannot believe what he is saying. He has always been such a kind and caring person. He is such a good father to our children." She continued, "How could he do this to us?"

I listened as she described their twelve years of marriage. It was a story I had heard many times before. They had an exciting courtship, got married at the height of the "in love" experience, had the typical adjustments in the early days of marriage, and pursued the American dream. In due time, they came down off the emotional high of the "in love" experience but did not learn to speak each other's love language sufficiently. She had lived with a love tank only half full for the last several years, but she had received enough expressions of love to make her think everything was okay. However, his love tank was empty.

I told Becky I would see if Brent would talk with me. I told Brent on the phone, "As you know, Becky came to see me and told me about her struggle with what is happening in the marriage. I want to help her, but in order to do so, I need to know what you are thinking."

He agreed readily, and now he sat in my office. His outward appearance was in stark contrast to Becky's. She had been weeping uncontrollably, but he was stoic. I had the impression, however, his weeping had taken place weeks or perhaps months ago, and it had been an inward weeping. The story Brent told confirmed my hunch.

"I just don't love her anymore," he said. "I haven't loved her for a long time. I don't want to hurt her, but we are not close. Our relationship has become empty. I don't enjoy being with her anymore. I don't know what happened. I wish it were different, but I don't have any feelings for her."

Brent was thinking and feeling what hundreds of thousands of husbands have thought and felt through the years. It's the "I don't love her anymore" mindset that gives men the emotional freedom to seek love with someone else. The same is true for wives who use the same excuse.

I sympathized with Brent, for I have been there. Thousands of husbands and wives have been there— emotionally empty, wanting to do the right thing, not wanting to hurt anyone, but being pushed by their emotional needs to seek love outside the marriage. Fortunately, I had discovered in the earlier years of my own

★ ★ ★

Meeting my wife's need for love is a choice I make each day.

marriage the difference between the "in love" experience and the "emotional need" to feel loved. Most in our society have not yet learned that difference.

The "in love" experience we discussed in chapter 3 is on the level of instinct. It's not premeditated; it simply happens in the normal context of male-female relationships. It can be fostered or quenched, but it does not arise by conscious choice. It is short-lived (usually two years or less) and seems to serve for humankind the same function as the mating call of the Canada goose.

The "in love" experience temporarily meets one's emotional need for love. It gives us the feeling someone cares, someone admires us and appreciates us. Our emotions soar with the thought that another person sees us as number one, that he or she is willing to devote time and energies exclusively to our relationship. For a brief period, however long it lasts, our emotional need for love is met. Our tank is full; we can conquer the world. Nothing is impossible. For many individuals, it's the first time they have ever lived with a full emotional tank, and it's euphoric.

In time, however, we come down from that natural high back to the real world. If our spouse has learned to speak our primary love language, our need for love will continue to be satisfied. If, on the other hand, he or she does not speak our love language, our tank will slowly drain, and we will no longer feel loved. Meeting that need in one's spouse is definitely a choice. If I learn the emotional love language of my spouse and speak it frequently, she will continue to feel loved. When she comes down from the obsession of the "in love" experience, she will hardly even miss it because her emotional love tank will continue to be filled. However, if I have not learned her primary love language or have chosen not to speak it, when she descends from the emotional high, she will have the natural yearnings of unmet emotional need. After some years of living with an empty love tank, she will likely "fall in love" with someone else, and the cycle will begin again.

Meeting my wife's need for love is a choice I make each day. If I know her primary love language and choose to speak it, her deepest emotional need will be met and she will feel secure in my love. If she does the same for me, my emotional needs are met and both of us live with a full tank. In a state of emotional contentment, both of us will give our creative energies to many wholesome projects outside the marriage while we continue to keep our marriage exciting and growing.

With all of that in my mind, I looked back at the deadpan face of Brent and wondered if I could help him. I knew in my heart he was probably already involved with another "in love" experience. I wondered if it was in the beginning stages or at its height. Few men suffering from an empty emotional love tank leave their marriage until they have prospects of meeting that need somewhere else.

Brent was honest and revealed he had been in love with someone else for several months. He had hoped the feelings would go away and he could work things out with his wife. But things at home had gotten worse, and his love for the other woman had increased. He could not imagine living without his new lover.

I sympathized with Brent in his dilemma. He sincerely did not want to hurt his wife or his children, but at the same time, he felt he deserved a life of happiness. I told him the dismal statistics on second marriages. He was surprised to hear that but was certain he would beat the odds. I told him about the research on the effects of divorce on children, but he was convinced he would continue to be a good father to his children and they would get over the trauma of the divorce. I talked to Brent about the issues in this book and explained the difference between the experience of falling in love and the deep emotional need to feel loved. I explained the 5 Love Languages and challenged him to give his marriage another chance. All the while, I knew my intellectual

★ ★ ★

Almost never do two people fall in love on the same day, and almost never do they fall out of love on the same day.

and reasoned approach to marriage compared to the emotional high he was experiencing was like pitting a BB gun against an automatic weapon. He expressed appreciation for my concern and asked that I do everything possible to help Becky. But he assured me he saw no hope for the marriage.

One month later, I received a call from Brent. He indicated he would like to talk with me again. This time when he entered my office, he was noticeably disturbed. He was not the calm, cool man I had seen before. His lover had begun to come down off the emotional high, and she was observing things in Brent she did not like. She was withdrawing from the relationship, and he was crushed. Tears came to his eyes as he told me how much she meant to him and how unbearable it was to experience her rejection.

I listened for an hour before Brent ever asked for my advice. I told him how sympathetic I was to his pain and indicated that what he was experiencing was the natural emotional grief from a loss, and that the grief would not go away overnight. I explained, however, that the experience was inevitable. I reminded him of the temporary nature of the "in love" experience, that sooner or later, we always come down from the high to the real world. Some fall out of love before they get married; others, after they get married. He agreed it was better now than later.

After a while, I suggested that perhaps the crisis was a good time for him and his wife to get some marriage counseling. I reminded him that true, long-lasting emotional love is a choice and that emotional love could be reborn in his marriage if he and his wife learned to love each other in the right love languages. He agreed to marriage counseling, and nine months later, Brent and Becky left my office with a reborn marriage. When I saw Brent three years later, he told me what a wonderful marriage he had and thanked me for helping him at a crucial time in his life. He told me the grief over losing the other lover had been gone for more than two years. He smiled and said, "My tank has never been so full, and Becky is the happiest woman you are ever going to meet."

Fortunately Brent was the benefactor of what I call the disequilibrium of the "in love" experience. That is, almost never do two people fall in love on the same day, and almost never do they fall out of love on the same day. You don't have to be a social scientist to discover that truth. Just listen to country music. Brent's lover happened to have fallen out of love at an opportune time.

★ ★ ★

Love is something you do for someone else, not something you do for yourself.

## ACTIONS AND EMOTIONS

During the nine months I counseled Brent and Becky, we worked through numerous conflicts they had never resolved before. But the key to the rebirth of their marriage was discovering each other's primary love language and choosing to speak it frequently.

"What if the love language of your spouse is something that doesn't come naturally for you?" I am often asked this question at my marriage seminars, and my answer is, "So?"

My wife's love language is "Acts of Service." One of the things I do for her regularly as an act of love is to vacuum the floors. Do you think vacuuming floors comes naturally for me? My mother used to make me vacuum. All through junior high and high school, I couldn't go play ball on Saturday until I finished vacuuming the entire house. In those days, I said to myself, "When I get out of here, one thing I am not going to do: I am not going to vacuum houses. I'll get myself a wife to do that."

But I vacuum our house now, and I vacuum it regularly. And there is only one reason I vacuum our house. Love. You couldn't pay me enough to vacuum a house, but I do it for love. You see, when an action doesn't come naturally to you, it's a greater expression of love. My wife knows that when I vacuum the house, it's nothing but 100 percent pure, unadulterated love, and I get credit for the whole thing!

Someone says, "But, Dr. Chapman, that's different. I know my spouse's love language is physical touch, and I am not a toucher. I never saw my mother and father hug each other. They never hugged me. I am just not a toucher. What am I going to do?"

Do you have two hands? Can you put them together? Now, imagine you have your spouse in the middle and pull him/her toward you. I'll bet if you hug your spouse three thousand times, it will begin to feel more comfortable. But ultimately, comfort is not the issue. We are talking about love, and love is something you do for someone else, not something you do for yourself. Most of us do many things each day that do not come "naturally" for us. For some of us, that is getting out of bed in the morning. We go against our feelings and get out of bed. Why? Because we believe there is something worthwhile to do that day. And normally, before the day is over, we feel good about having gotten up. Our actions preceded our emotions.

The same is true with love. We discover the primary love language of our spouse, and we choose to speak it whether or not it is natural for us. We are not claiming to have warm, excited feelings. We are simply choosing to do it for his or her benefit. We want to meet our spouse's emotional need, and we reach out to speak his love language. In so doing, his emotional love tank is filled and chances are he will reciprocate and speak our language. When he does, our emotions return, and our love tank begins to fill.

Love is a choice. And either partner can start the process today.

## YOUR TURN

*A key thought here is the idea of speaking our mate's love language whether or not it is natural for us. Why is this so fundamental to a healthy marriage?*

# THE 5 LOVE LANGUAGES®

# CHAPTER 12

# Loving *the* Unlovely

It was a beautiful September Saturday. My wife and I were strolling through Reynolda Gardens, enjoying the flora, some of which had been imported from around the world. The gardens had originally been developed by R. J. Reynolds, the tobacco magnate, as a part of his country estate. They are now a part of the Wake Forest University campus. We had just passed the rose garden when I noticed Ann, a woman who had begun counseling two weeks earlier, approaching us. She was looking down at the cobblestone walkway and appeared to be in deep thought. When I greeted her, she was startled but looked up and smiled. I introduced her to Karolyn, and we exchanged pleasantries. Then, without any lead-in, she asked me one of the most profound questions I have ever heard: "Dr. Chapman, is it possible to love someone whom you hate?"

I knew the question was born of deep hurt and deserved a thoughtful answer. I knew I would be seeing her the following week for another counseling appointment, so I said, "Ann, that is one of the most thought-provoking questions I have ever heard. Why don't we discuss that next week?" She agreed, and Karolyn and I continued our stroll. But Ann's question did not go away. Later, as we drove home, Karolyn and I discussed it. We reflected on the early days of our own marriage and remembered that we had often experienced feelings of hate. Our condemning words to each other had brought us hurt and, on the heels of hurt, anger. And anger held inside becomes hate.

What made the difference for us? We both knew it was the choice to love. We had realized that if we continued our pattern of demanding and condemning, we would destroy our marriage. Fortunately over a period of about a year, we had learned how to discuss our differences without condemning each other, how to make decisions without destroying our unity, how to give constructive suggestions without being demanding, and eventually how to speak each other's primary love language. Our choice to love was made in the midst of negative feelings toward each other. When we started speaking each other's primary love language, the feelings of anger and hate abated.

★ ★ ★

I surmised that perhaps her only hope for marital survival was in her faith.

Our situation, however, was different from Ann's. Karolyn and I had both been open to learning and growing. I knew Ann's husband was not. She had told me the previous week she had begged him to go for counseling. She had pleaded for him to read a book or listen to a speaker on marriage, but he had refused all her efforts toward growth. According to her, his attitude was, "I don't have any problems. You are the one with the problems." In his mind he was right, she was wrong— it was as simple as that. Her feelings of love for him had been killed through the years by his constant criticism and condemnation. After ten years of marriage, her emotional energy was depleted and her self-esteem almost destroyed. Was there hope for Ann's marriage? Could she love an unlovely husband? Would he ever respond in love to her?

## LOVE'S GREATEST CHALLENGE

I knew Ann was a deeply religious person and she attended church regularly. I surmised that perhaps her only hope for marital survival was in her faith. The next day, with Ann in mind, I began to read Luke's account of the life of Christ. I have always admired Luke's writing because he was a physician who gave attention to details and in the first century wrote an orderly account of the teachings and lifestyle of Jesus of Nazareth. In what many have called Jesus' greatest sermon, I read the following words, which I call love's greatest challenge.

> *I tell you who hear me: Love your enemies, do good to those who hate you, bless those who curse you, pray for those who mistreat you. . . . Do to others as you would have them do to you. If you love those who love you, what credit is that to you? Even "sinners" love those who love them.*[4]

It seemed to me that that profound challenge, written almost two thousand years ago, might be the direction that Ann was looking for, but could she do it? Could anyone do it? Is it possible to love a spouse who has become your enemy? Is it possible to love one who has cursed you, mistreated you, and expressed feelings of contempt and hate for you? And if she could, would there

★ ★ ★

"I just don't know if I can ever love him again after all he has done to me."

be any payback? Would her husband ever change and begin to express love and care for her? I was astounded by this further word from Jesus' sermon: "Give, and it will be given to you. A good measure, pressed down, shaken together and running over, will be poured into your lap. For with the measure you use, it will be measured to you."[5]

Could that principle of loving an unlovely person possibly work in a marriage as far gone as Ann's? I decided to do an experiment. I would take as my hypothesis that if Ann could learn her husband's primary love language and speak it for a period of time so that his emotional need for love was met, eventually he would reciprocate and begin to express love to her. I wondered, *Would it work?*

I met with Ann the next week and listened again as she reviewed the hurts in her marriage. At the end of her synopsis, she repeated the question she had asked in Reynolda Gardens. This time she put it in the form of a statement: "Dr. Chapman, I just don't know if I can ever love him again after all he has done to me."

"Have you talked about your situation with any of your friends?" I asked.

"With two of my closest friends," she said, "and a little bit with some other people."

"And what was their response?"

"'Get out,'" she said. "They all tell me to get out, that he will never change, and that I am simply prolonging the agony. But I just can't bring myself to do that. Maybe I should, but I just can't believe that's the right thing to do."

"It seems to me that you are torn between your religious and moral beliefs that tell you it is wrong to get out of the marriage, and your emotional pain, which tells you that getting out is the only way to survive," I said.

"That's exactly right, Dr. Chapman. I don't know what to do."

"I am deeply sympathetic with your struggle," I continued. "You are in a very difficult situation. I wish I could offer you an easy answer. Unfortunately, I can't. Both of the alternatives you mentioned, getting out or staying in, will likely bring you a great deal of pain. Before you make that decision, I do have one idea. I am not sure it will work, but I'd like you to try it. I know from what you have told me your religious faith is important to you and that you have a great deal of respect for the teachings of Jesus."

She nodded affirmingly. I continued, "I want to read something Jesus once said that has some application to your marriage." I read slowly and deliberately.

> *"I tell you who hear me: Love your enemies, do good to those who hate you, bless those who curse you, pray for those who mistreat you. . . . Do to others as you would have them do to you. If you love those who love you, what credit is that to you? Even 'sinners' love those who love them."*

"Does that sound like your husband? Has he treated you as an enemy rather than as a friend?"

She nodded.

"Has he ever cursed you?" I asked.

"Many times."

"Has he ever mistreated you?"

"Often."

"And has he told you he hates you?"

"Yes."

## THE SIX-MONTH EXPERIMENT

"Ann, if you are willing, I would like to do an experiment. I would like to see what would happen if we apply this principle to your marriage. Let me explain what I mean." I went on to explain to Ann the concept of the emotional tank and the fact that when the tank is low, as hers was, we have no love feelings toward our spouse but simply experience emptiness and pain. Since love is such a deep emotional need, the lack of it is perhaps our deepest emotional pain. I told her if we could learn to speak each other's primary love language, that emotional need could be met and positive feelings could grow again.

"Does that make sense to you?" I inquired.

"Dr. Chapman, you have just described my life. I have never seen it so clearly before. We were in love before we got married, but not long after our marriage, we came down off the high and we never learned to speak each other's love language. My tank has been empty for years, and I am sure his has also. Dr. Chapman, if I had understood this concept earlier, maybe none of this would have happened."

"We can't go back, Ann," I said. "All we can do is try to make the future different. I would like to propose a six-month experiment."

"I'll try anything," Ann said.

I liked her positive spirit, but I wasn't sure whether she understood how difficult the experiment would be.

"Let's begin by stating our objective," I said. "If in six months you could have your fondest wish, what would it be?"

Ann sat in silence for some time. Then thoughtfully she said, "I would like to see Glenn loving me again and expressing it by spending time with me. I would like to see us doing things together, going places together. I would like to feel he is interested in my world. I would like to see us talking when we go out to eat. I'd like him to listen to me. I'd like to feel he values my ideas. I would like to see us taking trips together and having fun again. I would like to know he values our marriage more than anything."

Ann paused and then continued. "On my part, I would like to have warm, positive feelings toward him again. I would like to gain respect for him again. I would like to be proud of him. Right now, I don't have those feelings."

I was writing as Ann was speaking. When she finished, I read aloud what she had said. "That sounds like a pretty lofty objective," I said, "but is that really what you want, Ann?"

"Right now, that sounds like an impossible objective," Ann replied, "but more than anything, that's what I would like to see."

"Then let's agree," I said, "that this will be our objective. In six months, we want to see you and Glenn having this kind of love relationship.

"Now, let me suggest a hypothesis. The purpose of our experiment will be to prove whether or not the hypothesis is true. Let's hypothesize that if you could speak Glenn's primary love language consistently for a six-month period, somewhere along the line his emotional need for love would begin to be met; and as his emotional tank filled, he would begin to reciprocate love to you. That hypothesis is built upon the idea that the emotional need for love is our deepest emotional need; and when that need is being met, we tend to respond positively to the person who is meeting it."

I continued, "You understand that that hypothesis places all the initiative in your hands. Glenn is not trying to work on this marriage. You are. This hypothesis says if you can channel your energies in the right direction, there is a good possibility Glenn will eventually reciprocate." I read the other portion of Jesus' sermon recorded by Luke, the physician. "*Give, and it will be given to you. A good measure, pressed down, shaken together and running over, will be poured into your lap. For with the measure you use, it will be measured to you."*

"As I understand that, Jesus is stating a principle, not a way to manipulate people. Generally speaking, if we are kind and loving toward people, they will tend to be kind and loving toward us. That does not mean we can make a person kind by being kind to him. We are independent agents. Thus, we can spurn love and walk away from love or even spit into the face of love. There is no guarantee Glenn will respond to your acts of love. We can only say there is a good possibility he will do so." (A counselor can never predict with absolute certainty individual human behavior. Based on research and personality studies, a counselor can only predict how a person is likely to respond in a given situation.)

After we agreed on the hypothesis, I said to Ann, "Now let's discuss your and Glenn's primary love languages. I'm assuming from what you have told me already that quality time may be your primary love language. What do you think?"

"I think so, Dr. Chapman. In the early days when we spent time together and Glenn listened to me, we spent long hours talking together, doing things together. I really felt loved. More than anything, I wish that part of our marriage could return. When we spend time together, I feel like he really cares, but when he's always doing other things, I feel like his work and other pursuits are more important than our relationship."

"And what do you think Glenn's primary love language is?" I inquired.

"I think it's physical touch and especially the sexual part of the marriage. I know that when I felt more loved by him and we were more sexually active, he had a different attitude. I think that's his primary love language."

"Does he ever complain about the way you talk to him?"

"Well, he says I nag him all the time. He also says I don't support him, that I'm always against his ideas."

"Then let's assume," I said, "that physical touch is his primary love language and words of affirmation is his secondary love language. The reason I suggest the second is that if he complains about negative words, apparently positive words would be meaningful to him.

"Now, let me suggest a plan to test our hypothesis. What if you go home and say to Glenn, 'I've been thinking about us and I've decided that I would like to be a better wife to you. So if you have any suggestions as to how I could be a better wife, I want you to know I am open to them. You can tell me now or you can think about it first, but I would really like to work on being a better wife.' Whatever his response, negative or positive, simply accept it as information. That initial statement lets him know that something different is about to happen in your relationship.

"Then based upon your guess that his primary love language is physical touch and my suggestion that his secondary love language may be words of affirmation, focus your attention on those two areas for one month.

"If Glenn comes back with a suggestion as to how you might be a better wife, accept that information and work it into your plan. Look for positive things in Glenn's life and give him verbal affirmation about those things. In the meantime, stop all verbal complaints. If you want to complain about something, write it down in your personal notebook rather than saying anything about it to Glenn this month.

"Begin taking more initiative in physical touch and sexual involvement. Surprise him by being aggressive, not simply responding to his advances. Set a goal to have sexual intercourse at least once a week the first two weeks and twice a week the following two weeks." Ann had told me she and Glenn had had sexual intercourse only once or twice in the past six months. I figured this plan would get things off dead center rather quickly.

"Oh, Dr. Chapman, this is going to be difficult," Ann said. "I have found it hard to be sexually responsive to him when he ignores me all the time. I have felt used rather than loved in our sexual encounters. He acts as though I am totally unimportant all the rest of the time and then wants to jump in bed and use my body. I have resented that, and I guess that's why we have not had sex very often in the last few years."

"Your response has been natural and normal," I assured Ann. "For most wives, the desire to be sexually intimate with their husbands grows out of a sense of being loved by their husbands. If they feel loved, then they desire sexual intimacy. If they do not feel loved, they likely feel used in the sexual context. That is why loving someone who is not loving you is extremely difficult. It goes against our natural tendencies. You will probably have to rely heavily upon your faith in God in order to do this. Perhaps it will help if you read again Jesus' sermon on loving your enemies, loving those who hate you, loving those who use you. And then ask God to help you practice the teachings of Jesus."

I could tell Ann was following what I was saying. Her eyes were bright and full of questions.

"But, Dr. Chapman, isn't it being hypocritical to express love sexually when you have such negative feelings toward the person?"

"Perhaps it would be helpful for us to distinguish between love as a feeling and love as an action," I said. "If you claim to have feelings you do not have, that is hypocritical and such false communication is not the way to build intimate relationships. But if you express an act of love designed for the other person's benefit or pleasure, it's simply a choice. You are not claiming the action grows out of a deep emotional bonding. You are simply choosing to do something for his benefit. I think that must be what Jesus meant.

"Certainly we do not have warm feelings for people who hate us. That would be abnormal, but we can do loving acts for them. That is simply a choice. We hope such loving acts will have a positive effect upon their attitudes and behavior and treatment, but at least we have chosen to do something positive for them."

My answer seemed to satisfy Ann, at least for the moment. I had the feeling we would discuss that again. I also had the feeling that if the experiment was going to get off the ground, it would be because of Ann's deep faith in God.

"After the first month," I said, "I want you to ask Glenn for feedback on how you are doing. Using your own words, ask him, 'Glenn, you remember a few weeks ago when I told you I was going to try to be a better wife? I want to ask how you think I am doing.'

"Whatever Glenn says, accept it as information. He may be sarcastic, he may be flippant or hostile, or he may be positive. Whatever his response, do not argue but accept it and assure him you are serious and you really want to be a better wife, and if he has additional suggestions, you are open to them.

"Follow this pattern of asking for feedback once a month for the entire six months. Whenever Glenn gives you the first positive response, you will know your efforts are getting through to him emotionally. One week after you receive the first positive feedback, I want you to make a request of Glenn—something you would like him to do, something in keeping with your primary love language. For example, you may say to him one evening, 'Glenn, do you know something I would like to do? Do you remember how we used to go take walks in Reynolda Gardens together? I'd like to go do that with you on Thursday night. The kids are going to be staying at my mom's. Do you think that would be possible?'

"Make the request something specific, not general. Don't say, 'You know, I wish we would spend more time together.' That's too vague. How will you know when he's done it? But if you make your request specific, he will know exactly what you want and you will know that, when he does it, he is choosing to do something for your benefit.

"Do this each month. If he does it, fine; if he doesn't do it, fine. But when he does it, you will know that he is responding to your needs. In the process, you are teaching him your primary love language because the requests you make are in keeping with your love language. If he chooses to begin loving you in your primary language, your positive emotions toward him will begin to resurface. Your emotional tank will begin to fill up and in time the marriage will, in fact, be reborn."

"Dr. Chapman, I would do anything if that could happen," Ann said.

"Well," I responded, "it will take a lot of hard work, but I believe it's worth a try. I'm personally interested to see if this experiment works and if our hypothesis is true. I would like to meet with you regularly throughout this process—perhaps every two weeks—and I would like you to keep records on the positive words of affirmation you give Glenn each week. Also, I would like you to bring me your list of complaints you have written in your notebook without stating them to Glenn. Perhaps from the felt complaints, I can help you build specific requests for Glenn that will help meet some of those frustrations. Eventually, I want you to learn how to share your frustrations and irritations in a constructive way, and I want you and Glenn to learn how to work through those irritations and conflicts. But during this six-month experiment, I want you to write them down without telling Glenn."

Ann left, and I believed she had the answer to her question: "Is it possible to love someone whom you hate?"

In the next six months, Ann saw a tremendous change in Glenn's attitude and treatment of her. The first month, he treated the whole thing lightly. But after the second month, he gave her positive feedback about her efforts. In the last four months, he responded positively to almost all of her requests, and her feelings for him began to change drastically. Glenn never came for counseling, but he did listen to some of my CDs and discuss them with Ann. He encouraged Ann to continue her counseling, which she did for another three months after our experiment. To this day, Glenn swears to his friends I am a miracle worker. I know in fact that love is a miracle worker.

Perhaps you need a miracle in your own marriage. Why not try Ann's experiment? Tell your spouse you have been thinking about your marriage and have decided you would like to do a better job of meeting his/her needs. Ask for suggestions on how you could improve. His suggestions will be a clue to his primary love language. If he makes no suggestions, guess his love language based on the things he has complained about over the years. Then, for six months, focus your attention on that love language. At the end of each month, ask your spouse for feedback on how you are doing and for further suggestions.

Whenever your spouse indicates he is seeing improvement, wait one week and then make a specific request. The request should be something you really want him to do for you. If he chooses to do it, you will know that he is responding to your needs. If he does not honor your request, continue to love him. Maybe next month he will respond positively. If your spouse starts speaking your love language by responding to your requests, your positive emotions toward him will return, and in time your marriage will be reborn. I cannot guarantee the results, but scores of people whom I have counseled have experienced the miracle of love.

## YOUR TURN

*If your marriage is in the serious trouble discussed in this chapter, you need to begin by making a strong commitment of the will to undertake the following experiment. You risk further pain and rejection, but you also stand to regain a healthy and fulfilling marriage. Count the cost; it's worth the attempt.*

1. *Ask how you can be a better spouse, and regardless of the other's attitude, act on what he or she tells you.*

2. *When you receive positive feedback, you know there is progress. Each month make one nonthreatening but specific request that is easy for your spouse. Make sure it relates to your primary love language and will help replenish your empty tank.*

3. *When your spouse responds and meets your need, you will be able to react with not only your will but your emotions as well. Without overreacting, continue positive feedback and affirmation of your spouse at these times.*

4. *As your marriage begins to truly heal and grow deeper, make sure you don't "rest on your laurels" and forget your spouse's love language and daily needs. You're on the road to your dreams, so stay there! Put appointments into your schedule to assess together how you're doing.*

# THE 5 LOVE LANGUAGES®

# CHAPTER 13

# A Personal Word

Well, what do you think? Having read these pages, walked in and out of the lives of several couples, visited small villages and large cities, sat with me in the counseling office, and talked with people in restaurants, what do you think? Could these concepts radically alter the emotional climate of your marriage? What would happen if you discovered the primary love language of your spouse and chose to speak it consistently?

Neither you nor I can answer that question until you have tried it. I know many military couples who have heard this concept at my marriage seminars say that choosing to love and expressing it in the primary love language of their spouse has made a drastic difference in their marriage. When the emotional need for love is met, it creates a climate where the couple can deal with the rest of life in a much more productive manner. Consider Mark and Robin. Robin figured out that Mark's primary love language was affirming words, usually involving something specific ("I like how you're protective of me; it makes me feel loved"). "Knowing his love language greatly helps me understand him," she said. "Now, that's not to imply I always say the right thing! But simply knowing how he's wired has drawn us closer." Robin says her love language is acts of service. "Mark would compliment me about something, because that's his love language, and somehow it never made me feel all that great. But when we figured out that what I really valued were acts of service, even something small like bringing me coffee in bed in the morning, our marriage took a giant step."

We each come to marriage with a different personality and history. We bring emotional baggage into our marriage relationship. We come with different expectations, different ways of approaching things, and different opinions about what matters in life. In a healthy marriage, that variety of perspectives must be processed. We need not agree on everything, but we must find a way to handle our differences so they do not become divisive. With empty love tanks, couples tend to argue and withdraw, and some may tend to be violent verbally or physically in their arguments. But when the love tank is full, we create a climate of friendliness, a climate that seeks to understand, that is willing to allow differences and to negotiate problems. No single area of marriage affects the rest of marriage as much as meeting the emotional need for love.

> ★ ★ ★
>
> We need not agree on everything, but we must find a way to handle our differences so they do not become divisive.

The ability to love, especially when your spouse is not loving you, may seem impossible for some. Such love may require us to draw on our spiritual resources. A number of years ago, as I faced my own marital struggles, I rediscovered my spiritual roots. Having been raised in the

Christian tradition, I reexamined the life of Christ. When I heard Him praying for those who were killing Him, "Father, forgive them, for they know not what they do," I knew that I wanted that kind of love. I committed my life to Him and have found that He provides the inner spiritual energy to love, even when love is not reciprocated.

The high divorce rate in military marriages bears witness that thousands of couples have been living with an empty emotional love tank. I believe the concepts in this book could make a significant impact upon the marriages and families of military couples.

For those of you who have children, let me encourage you to discover your child's love language and speak it regularly. You can learn their language by the time they are three or four years old by observing their behavior. If they are regularly jumping into your lap and hugging you, their language is physical touch. If they say, "Come into my room, I want to show you something," they are asking for quality time.

All parents love their children, but not all children feel loved. For further help, see *The 5 Love Languages of Children*. There I discuss how love interfaces with the child's anger, with discipline, and learning.

It is my hope that *The 5 Love Languages Military Edition* will help military couples who have experienced the "in love" euphoria, who entered marriage with lofty dreams of making each other supremely happy but in the reality of day-to-day life are in danger of losing that dream entirely. I hope thousands of those couples will not only rediscover their dream but will see the path to making their dreams come true.

I dream of a day when the potential of the married couples in the military can be unleashed for the good of humankind, when husbands and wives can live life with full emotional love tanks and reach out to accomplish their potential as individuals and as couples. I dream of a day when children can grow up in homes filled with love and security, where children's developing energies can be channeled to learning and serving rather than seeking the love they did not receive at home. It is my desire that this brief volume will kindle the flame of love in your marriage and in the marriages of thousands of other military couples like you.

I wrote this for you. I hope it changes your life. And if it does, be sure to give it to someone else. I would be pleased if you would give a copy of this book to your family, to your brothers and sisters, to your married children, to your friends, and to other military couples. Who knows? Together we may see our dream come true.

For a free online study guide, please visit:

http://www.5lovelanguages.com

This group discussion guide is designed to both help couples apply the concepts from *The 5 Love Languages* and stimulate genuine dialogue among study groups.

# THE 5 LOVE LANGUAGES®

# CHAPTER 14

# Frequently Asked Questions

### 1. What if I cannot discover my primary love language?

"I've taken the Love Language Profile and my scores come out almost even except for Receiving Gifts. I know that's not my love language."

In the book, I discuss three approaches to discovering your love language on pages 153–54.

If, after reviewing those, you're still unsure, consider the example of one husband who told me he discovered his love language by simply following the process of elimination. He knew Receiving Gifts was not his language so he asked himself, "If I had to give up one of the remaining four, which one would I give up?" He concluded that apart from sexual intercourse, he could give up Physical Touch and Quality Time. This left Acts of Service and Words of Affirmation. While he appreciated the things his wife did for him, he knew her affirming words were really what gave him life. Thus, Words of Affirmation was his primary love language and Acts of Service his secondary love language.

## 2. What if I cannot discover my spouse's love language?

"My husband hasn't read the book, but we have discussed the love languages. He says he doesn't know what his love language is."

My first suggestion is to give him a copy of *The 5 Love Languages Men's Edition*. Since it is geared specifically to husbands, he is more likely to read it. If he reads it, he will be eager to share his love language with you. However, if he is unwilling to read the book, I would suggest you answer the three questions below:

1. How does he most often express love to others?
2. What does he complain about most often?
3. What does he request most often?

Though our spouse's complaints normally irritate us, they are actually giving us valuable information. If a spouse says, "We don't ever spend any time together," you may be tempted to say, "What do you mean? We went out to dinner Thursday night." Such a defensive statement will end the conversation. However, if you respond, "What would you like for us to do?" you will likely get an answer. The complaints of your spouse are the most powerful indicators of the primary love language.

You also might want to try a five-week experiment. The first week, you focus on one of the five love languages and seek to speak it every day and observe the response of your spouse. On Saturday and Sunday, you relax. The second week—Monday through Friday—you focus on another of the love languages and continue with a different language each of the five weeks. On the week you are speaking your spouse's primary love language, you are likely to see a difference in their countenance and the way they respond to you. It will be obvious that this is their primary love language.

### 3. My husband's military style of communicating hurts me. How can I help him understand this?

"Due to how the Army environment 'trains' its soldiers, my husband's tone and words are often harsh, exasperated, negative, or sarcastic. He says his comments are not aimed at me, but it is hard not to take them that way when I listen so closely for words of affirmation."

I am deeply sympathetic with your question. Because your love language is Words of Affirmation, harsh, critical words will hurt you more deeply than they would hurt someone who has a different love language. My first suggestion is to learn your husband's primary love language and speak it regularly for two months while making no comments about his harsh words to you. After two months, ask the question, "On a scale of 0 to 10, how full is your love tank?" or "How much love do you feel coming from me?" When he gives you an 8, 9, or 10, then you are in a position to have a positive influence on his behavior.

Now that he feels your love, you are ready to help him understand how deeply his harsh words hurt you. If his primary love language is Quality Time, you say to him, "I hope you know how much I love you. I want to ask you a personal question. If I withdrew from you and ignored you, and stopped spending time with you, and refused to take walks with you, how would you feel?" He may well say, "I would feel extremely unloved by you." Then you say, "That's exactly how I feel when you speak harsh, critical words to me. My love language is Words of Affirmation, and when you use words in a negative way, they cut me very deeply and make me feel you don't love me. I know you use harsh words every day at work, but I'm asking that you please make an effort to speak to me as a wife and not one of your men."

If his love language is Physical Touch, you would take the same approach and after he assures you he feels loved by you, you would say to him, "I hope you know how much I love you. I want to ask you a personal question. If I stopped reaching out and touching you, if I refused to hold hands with you and drew back when you tried to kiss me and withdrew when you wanted to have sexual intercourse, how would that make you feel?" Once he responds, then you tell him that's how deeply you hurt when he uses harsh, loud words when speaking to you. You would take the same approach whatever his primary love language is. This approach helps him understand how deeply you feel hurt by his negative, sarcastic, harsh words, and he is very likely to change his behavior.

## 4. How do we speak our spouse's love language when our own love tank is empty?

"I am burned out from years of intense deployment cycles. It's hard to desire to speak my spouse's love language, when mine is not being spoken. I want to desire to do that again, but I'm just so tired. How do we regain the passion in fulfilling the love language of our husbands?"

I am certain that wives who have gone through numerous deployments can identify with your question. Physically and emotionally, we become drained with all the responsibilities upon us while they are deployed and when we are receiving very little love from our spouses. That is why I have recommended throughout this book that you learn how to speak each other's love language while you are apart, so you can keep emotional love alive in the relationship. That is the ideal.

However, I know your husband may not even be familiar with the love language concept. My first suggestion is to put a copy of this book in his hands and ask him to read the first chapter and let you know what he thinks of it. Most men who read the first chapter will end up reading the entire book and will find themselves motivated to reach out and communicate love to their wives.

It is always easier to love someone who is loving you. However, someone must start the process. Since you have read this book, and perhaps already know your husband's love language, my suggestion is that you make a conscious choice to speak his love language at least twice a week for the next three months and see what happens. My prediction is that at the end of the three months, his love tank is getting full and you can make a legitimate request of him. "Do you know what would make me happy?" or "Do you know what I would really like?" and you share with him some expression of your love language that would be meaningful to you. Because he feels loved by you, he is far more likely to respond to your request. I know to take this approach will require you to rise above your emotional, physical, sense of fatigue. But I can assure you it is worth the effort.

## 5. I'm married to the military. When the government calls, I have to answer. How can my wife and I deal with this issue?

"My wife's love language is Quality Time, and I know she hates it when I take work phone calls during our dates. But I have no choice—I took an oath to the military and have to be on call all the time as part of my current assignment."

You are reading your wife well. It is true that for those who have Quality Time as their love language, they are hurt and annoyed when you divert your attention from your time together to answer a phone call. I understand your commitment to the military. My suggestion would be to look at the phone when it rings, determine if it is a military call or a call from one of your friends unrelated to the military. You answer only the calls related to your military duty, and you do not answer other calls. These will be recorded in your voicemail and you can answer them after the date is over. Many of us are much too glued to our phones. There was a day, you may remember, when we did not have cell phones and our times together at a restaurant were never interrupted by a phone. We seem to have survived rather well in those days. I applaud the convenience of cell phones, but we must make our own rules as to how they will be used so as to enhance our marital relationship, rather than detracting from it.

### 6. How do we find ways to communicate when we have both changed from long deployments and feel like strangers to each other?

When you first met and started dating, likely neither of you knew each other very well. How did you get to know each other and come to the place where you decided to marry? My guess is that you had many long conversations asking each other questions about their past and present. Essentially, communication is talking and listening. But questions are a key tool to open the heart and mind of the other person. Here are some suggested questions:

1. When you were a child, what kind of relationship did you have with your mother? Father? Brothers or sisters? (Don't ask all of these in the same conversation.)
2. What could I do to make your life easier?
3. What one thing could I change that would make me a better wife? or, husband?

4. Did you meet any new people at work today?

5. What was the biggest challenge you faced while on duty today?

6. Of all the people you interact with on a regular basis, whom do you like the most and why?

Such questions tend to make it easier for your spouse to respond. Some time ago I wrote a larger collection of such questions in a little booklet entitled *101 Conversation Starters for Couples*. You can find it on Amazon or at a local retailer.

The second suggestion is for the two of you to establish a weekly date night in which the two of you go out for dinner, and agree beforehand that each of you will tell one event that was humorous while the two of you were apart, and one event that was very painful while the two of you were apart. Often, those who have been deployed are reluctant to talk about their experiences. But when you limit the conversation to one positive and one negative experience, they are less likely to be overwhelmed. Once your spouse shares the negative event, you may say, "That must have been extremely hard for you." If they respond, listen carefully and affirm their feelings. "I can see how you would have felt that way. I'm sure that was far more painful than I can imagine."

My third suggestion is that when you are together you have a daily sharing time in which each of you shares with the other—two things that happened in my life today and how I feel about them. These may be positive experiences or negative experiences. You are sharing events that happen in your life, and you are sharing your emotional response. You are building both intellectual and emotional intimacy.

Building intimacy after long deployments is a slow process. It cannot be rushed. But when you become adept at asking questions, and adept at revealing past experiences with each other, you are building a platform on which you can continue to build intimacy: intellectually, socially, physically, and spiritually.

### 7. Does combat trauma trump love languages?

"I have PTSD and am completely overwhelmed by the idea of speaking love languages. I have enough to deal with on my own. Can't I get a break until I feel more up to it?"

Those who have never experienced PTSD find it hard to imagine the emotional, mental effect of traumatic stress. If your spouse has not attended classes to help them understand, or read books or explored websites to gain understanding about PTSD, I would suggest you encourage her to do so. This will make them more empathetic to what you are going through.

However, we cannot postpone love while we are going through the effects of PTSD. Actually, speaking each other's love language will help you in the process of recovering from traumatic stress. Our deepest emotional need is to feel loved. When we feel loved by our spouse, we are far more likely to handle the stresses of life than if we feel our spouse has rejected us. Giving and receiving love is the heart of life; all the rest is just background music. Therefore, I am suggesting that with whatever energy you have, you invest it in the best possible way in loving your spouse. If they reciprocate your love, you are indeed a fortunate man. When each of you feels secure in the love of the other, you can walk together through the difficulties created by PTSD.

### 8. Do the love languages work in other cultures?

Yes. These five fundamental ways of expressing love are universal. However, the dialects in which these languages are spoken will differ from culture to culture. For example, the kind of touches appropriate in one culture may not be appropriate in another. The Acts of Service spoken in one culture may not be spoken in another. But when these cultural adaptations are made, the concept of the five love languages will have a profound impact upon the couples in that culture.

## 9. What if I speak my spouse's love language and they don't respond?

"My husband would not read the book so I decided to speak his love language and see what would happen. Nothing happened. He didn't even acknowledge that I did anything differently. How long am I supposed to continue speaking his love language when there is no response?"

I know it can become discouraging when you feel you are investing in the marriage and receiving nothing in return. There are two possible reasons for this. First and most likely, you are speaking the wrong love language. Wives often assume their husband's love language is Physical Touch. In reality, his primary love language may be Words of Affirmation. Because she feels no love coming from him, she may be verbally critical of him. Her critical words are like daggers to his heart, so he withdraws from her. The problem is not her sincerity; the problem is she is actually speaking the wrong love language.

On the other hand, assuming you are speaking your spouse's primary love language, there is another reason why they may not be responding positively. If the spouse is already involved in another romantic relationship, either emotionally or sexually, they will often reason that your efforts have come too late. They may even perceive that your efforts are temporary and insincere and you are simply trying to manipulate them to stay in the marriage. Even if your spouse is not involved with someone else, if your relationship has been hostile for a long time, they may still perceive your efforts as being manipulative.

In this situation, the temptation is to give up, to stop speaking their love language because it is not making any difference. The worst thing you can do is to yield to this temptation. If you give up, it will confirm their conclusion that your efforts were designed to manipulate them. The best approach you can take is to continue to speak their love language on a regular basis no matter how they treat you. Set yourself a goal of six months, nine months, or a year. Your attitude is "Whatever their response, I'm going to love them in their love language over the long haul. If they walk away from me, they will walk away from someone who is loving them unconditionally." This attitude will keep you on a positive road even when you feel discouraged. There is nothing more powerful than to love your spouse even when they are not responding positively. Whatever the ultimate response of your spouse, you will have the satisfaction of knowing you have done everything you could do to restore your marriage. If your spouse eventually chooses to reciprocate your love, you will have demonstrated for yourself the power of unconditional love. And you will reap the benefits of the rebirth of mutual love.

## 10. Can love be reborn after sexual infidelity?

Nothing devastates marital intimacy more than sexual unfaithfulness. However, this does not mean the marriage is destined for divorce. If the offending party is willing to break off the extramarital involvement and do the hard work of rebuilding the marriage, there can be genuine restoration. In my own counseling, I have seen scores of couples who have experienced healing after sexual infidelity. It involves not only breaking off the extramarital affair but discovering what led to the affair. Success in restoration is a two-pronged approach. First, the offending party must be willing to explore their own personality, beliefs, and lifestyle that led them to the affair. There must be a willingness to change attitudes and behavior patterns. Second, the couple must be willing to take an honest look at the dynamics of their marriage and be open to replacing destructive patterns with positive patterns of integrity and sincerity. Both of these will normally require the help of a professional counselor.

Research indicates the couples who are most likely to survive sexual infidelity are those who receive both individual and marriage counseling. Understanding the five love languages and choosing to speak each other's language can help create an emotional climate in which the hard work of restoring the marriage can be successful.

An interactive version of this Personal Profile is
also available at www.5lovelanguages.com

THE 5 LOVE LANGUAGES®

# Profile *for* Husbands

Y ou may think you already know your primary love language. Then again, you may have no clue. The 5 Love Languages Profile will help you know for certain which love language is yours—Words of Affirmation, Quality Time, Receiving Gifts, Acts of Service, or Physical Touch.

The profile consists of 30 pairs of statements. You can only pick one statement in each pair as the one that best represents your desire. Read each pair of statements, and then, in the right-hand column, circle the letter that matches up with the statement you choose. It may be tough at times to decide between two statements, but you should only choose one per pair to ensure the most accurate profile results.

Allow at least 15 to 30 minutes to complete the profile. Take it when you are relaxed, and try not to rush through it. Once you've made your selections, go back and count the number of times you circled each individual letter. You can list the results in the appropriate spaces at the end of the profile.

Your wife may not do some of these, but if she did, which would you prefer?

1. I wish my wife would send me a love note (or text or email) for no special reason.  A

   I would like more hugs from my wife.  E

2. I would like to spend more time alone with my wife, just the two of us.  B

   I enjoy working around the house with my wife.  D

3. Receiving special gifts from my wife makes me happy—I wish she would do it more!  C

   One of my favorite things is traveling with my wife.  B

4. I would like my wife to run errands or put gas in my car.  D

   I wish my wife would touch me more.  E

5. I wish my wife would sometimes put her arm around me when we are with others.  E

   Every now and then I'd like to get a surprise gift from my wife.  C

6. I like going places with my wife—even the grocery store!  B

   I like to hold my wife's hand.  E

7. I value the gifts my wife gives me.  C

   I would love to hear my wife say the actual words "I love you" more often.  A

8. I wish my wife would sit close to me more often.  E

   I feel loved when my wife tells me, "You look good."  A

9. I wish my wife and I could spend more time together.  B

   Even the smallest gift from my wife is important to me.  C

10. I would love it if my wife could say, "I'm proud of you."  A

    When my wife cooks a nice meal for me, I feel very loved.  D

11. No matter what we do, I love doing things with my wife.  B

    I wish my wife would say more supportive things to me.  A

**12** Little things my wife does for me mean more to me than things she says. D

My wife and I need to hug more. E

**13** I would love to hear more praise from my wife. A

It means a lot to me when my wife gives me gifts I really like. C

**14** I wish my wife and I could spend more time together. B

I would like a back rub from my wife sometimes. E

**15** I wish my wife would be more enthusiastic about something I've accomplished. A

I wish my wife would help me with tasks, even those she dislikes. D

**16** I never get tired of my wife's kisses. E

I wish my wife would show more interest in things I like to do, even though they might not be her "thing." B

**17** I would like my wife to work with me on projects. D

I wish my wife would get more excited about gifts from me. C

**18** I love it when my wife compliments my appearance. A

I wish my wife wouldn't jump in to criticize my ideas rather than hearing me out. B

**19** I can't help but touch my wife when she's close by. E

I wish my wife would now and then run errands for me when I'm busy. D

**20** At times, when I'm feeling swamped at work, I wish my wife would see that and do more around the house. D

If my wife gives me a gift, I would like her to put thought into choosing it. C

**21** I wish my wife would give me her full attention when we're talking, and not look away or check her phone. B

Keeping the house clean is an important act of service. D

**22** I look forward to seeing what my wife gives me for my birthday. C

I know my wife loves me, but I wish she would tell me more often what I mean to her. A

23  It would be nice if when my wife takes a trip, she would bring me a little gift.  C

    I wish my wife would sometime surprise me by helping me with a chore I dislike.  D

24  It bothers me when my wife interrupts me.  B

    I never get tired of receiving gifts from my wife.  C

25  I want my wife to help me out when I'm tired.  D

    I wish my wife was as enthusiastic about going places as I am.  B

26  I love having sex with my wife.  E

    I like it when my wife goes to the store and picks up little things she knows I'll like.  C

27  I wish my wife would be more encouraging.  A

    I love to watch movies with my wife.  B

28  If I received a gift from my wife, I would feel appreciated.  C

    I just can't keep my hands off my wife.  E

29  I know my wife is busy, but sometimes I would love it if she would help me with things I have to do.  D

    I would really like it if my wife sometimes said, "I appreciate you."  A

30  I love embracing my wife after we've been apart for a while.  E

    I want to hear my wife say she believes in me.  A

A: _____ B: _____ C: _____ D: _____ E: _____

A = Words of Affirmation; B = Quality Time ; C = Receiving Gifts;
D = Acts of Service; E = Physical Touch

## INTERPRETING AND USING YOUR PROFILE SCORE

Your primary love language is the one that received the highest score. You are "bilingual" and have two primary love languages if point totals are equal for any two love languages. If your second highest scoring love language is close in score but not equal to your primary love language, then this simply means that both expressions of love are important to you. The highest possible score for any one love language is 12.

You may have scored certain ones of the love languages more highly than others, but do not dismiss those other languages as insignificant. Your wife may express love in those ways, and it will be helpful to you to understand this about her.

In the same way, it will benefit your wife to know your love language and express her affection for you in ways that you interpret as love. Every time you or your wife speak each other's language, you score emotional points with one another. Of course, this isn't a game with a scorecard! The payoff of speaking each other's love language is a greater sense of connection. This translates into better communication, increased understanding, and, ultimately, improved romance.

If your wife has not already done so, encourage her to take the 5 Love Languages Profile for Wives, which is available on page 209. Discuss your respective love languages, and use this insight to improve your marriage!

An interactive version of this Personal Profile is
also available at www.5lovelanguages.com

THE 5 LOVE LANGUAGES®

## THE 5 LOVE LANGUAGES
# Profile *for* Wives

Words of Affirmation, Quality Time, Receiving Gifts, Acts of Service, or Physical Touch? Which of these is your primary love language? The following profile will help you know for sure. Then you and your husband can discuss your respective love languages and use this information to improve your marriage!

The profile consists of 30 pairs of statements. You can only pick one statement in each pair as the one that best represents your desire. Read each pair of statements, and then, in the right-hand column, circle the letter that matches up with the statement you choose. It may be tough at times to decide between two statements, but you should only choose one per pair to ensure the most accurate profile results. Once you've finished making your selections, go back and count the number of times you circled each individual letter. List the results in the appropriate spaces at the end of the profile. Your primary love language is the one that receives the most points.

Your husband may not do some of these, but if he did, which would you prefer?

**1**
I would love to get a funny email from my husband.                                      A

I wish my husband would hug me more.                                                    E

**2**
I like to be alone with my husband.                                                     B

I wish sometime my husband would take my car to be washed, or do some other
act of service without being asked.                                                     D

**3**
I would love for my husband to bring me a special gift, no occasion needed.             C

I enjoy long trips with my husband.                                                     B

**4**
I would feel really loved if my husband did the laundry.                                D

I like it when my husband touches me.                                                   E

**5**
I would like my husband to put his arm around me sometimes when we are in public.       E

I wish my husband would bring me gifts when he travels.                                 C

**6**
I wish my husband was more enthusiastic about getting out and going places.             B

I like to hold my husband's hand.                                                       E

**7**
I feel loved when my husband gives me gifts.                                            C

I know he loves me, but I want to hear my husband say it.                               A

**8**
I like for my husband to sit close to me.                                               E

When I'm all dressed up, I wish my husband would compliment me.                         A

**9**
Spending time with my husband makes me happy.                                           B

I wish my husband would give me more small gifts that still mean something.             C

**10**
I would like to hear my husband say he's proud of me.                                   A

I wish my husband would help clean up without being told.                               D

**11**
No matter what we do, I love doing things with my husband.                              B

I would like to hear more supportive words from my husband.                             A

12  I wish my husband would not only say nice things to me, but do nice things for me.  D

I love to hug my husband.  E

13  I wish my husband would praise me more often.  A

I wish my husband would give me gifts that are more thoughtful and personal.  C

14  Just being around my husband makes me feel good.  B

I wish my husband would give me a massage.  E

15  If my husband would react positively to my accomplishments, that would be encouraging.  A

I wish my husband would help me with tasks that he doesn't enjoy—just because he knows it would mean a lot to me.  D

16  I never get tired of my husband's kisses.  E

I want my husband to show more interest in things I care about.  B

17  I feel loved when my husband helps me with projects.  D

I still get excited when opening a gift from my husband.  C

18  I wish my husband would compliment me on my appearance more often.  A

I want my husband to listen to me more and respect my ideas.  B

19  I can't help but touch my husband when he's close by.  E

When I have a lot of errands to run, I wish my husband would sometimes offer to help.  D

20  I would feel like giving my husband an award if he helped me around the house.  D

I would feel loved if my husband's gifts showed signs of thoughtfulness.  C

21  I wish my husband would give me his undivided attention when I'm talking to him and not play with his phone.  B

I would love for my husband to help clean the house.  D

22  I look forward to seeing what my husband gives me for my birthday.  C

I want to hear my husband say how much I mean to him.  A

**23**
I wish my husband gave me gifts more often.. — C
I wish my husband would help me, without my having to ask. — D

**24**
It bothers me when my husband interrupts me when I'm talking. — B
I never get tired of receiving gifts from my husband. — C

**25**
I would like for my husband to offer to help me when I'm tired. — D
It doesn't matter where we go, I just like going places with my husband. — B

**26**
I wish my husband and I cuddled more. — E
I wish my husband would surprise me with a gift more often. — C

**27**
My husband's encouraging words give me confidence. — A
I love to watch movies with my husband. — B

**28**
I wish my husband would give me a gift for no reason. — C
I love it it if my husband touched me more. — E

**29**
It means a lot to me when my husband helps me despite being busy. — D
I wish my husband would say, "I appreciate you." — A

**30**
I love embracing with my husband after we've been apart for a while. — E
I want to hear my husband say he misses me when I'm gone. — A

A: _____ B: _____ C: _____ D: _____ E: _____

A = Words of Affirmation; B = Quality Time; C = Receiving Gifts;
D = Acts of Service; E = Physical Touch

## INTERPRETING AND USING YOUR PROFILE SCORE

Your primary love language is the one that received the highest score. You are "bilingual" and have two primary love languages if point totals are equal for any two love languages. If your second highest scoring love language is close in score but not equal to your primary love language, then this simply means that both expressions of love are important to you. The highest possible score for any one love language is 12.

You may have scored certain of the love languages more highly than others, but do not dismiss those other languages as insignificant. Your husband may express love in those ways, and it will be helpful to you to understand this about him. In the same way, it will benefit your husband to know your love language and express his affection for you in ways that you interpret as love. Every time you or your husband speak each other's language, you score emotional points with one another. Of course, this isn't a game with a scorecard! The payoff of speaking each other's love language is a greater sense of connection. This translates into better communication, increased understanding, and, ultimately, improved romance.

# THE 5 LOVE LANGUAGES®

# Notes

1. US Bureau of the Census, Statistical Abstract of the United States, 122nd Ed. Washington, DC: US Government Printing Office, 2006.

2. Proverbs 18:21.

3. Proverbs 12:25.

4. Luke 6:27–28, 31–32.

5. Luke 6:38.

## STRENGTHEN YOUR RELATIONSHIPS.

## DISCOVER YOUR LOVE LANGUAGE

- Explore resources and tools
- Get free stuff
- Locate LIVE events
- Listen to podcasts
- Share your story
- Watch videos

Are you a military chaplain? If so, get free videos and learn about special discounts available under the *Free Tools* tab.

# GET CONNECTED!

**IMPROVING MILLIONS OF RELATIONSHIPS... ONE LANGUAGE AT A TIME.**
Receive practical love language applications, helpful tips to strengthen your relationships, links to relevant resources, and much more delivered straight to your inbox. Sign up for the FREE newsletter today at 5lovelanguages.com *(upper right corner of home page).*

Also, connect with Gary on your favorite social media platform.

/5lovelanguages    /drgarychapman    /drgarychapman    /user/drgarychapman

VISIT **5LoveLanguages.com**

# GIFTABLE RESOURCES

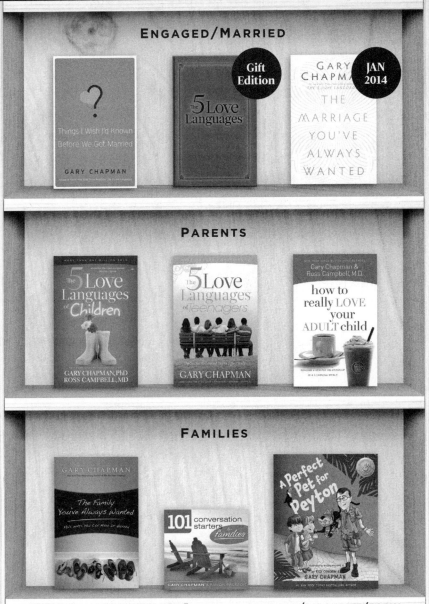

## ENGAGED/MARRIED

Things I Wish I'd Known Before We Got Married
GARY CHAPMAN

The 5 Love Languages — **Gift Edition**

GARY CHAPMAN — THE MARRIAGE YOU'VE ALWAYS WANTED — **JAN 2014**

## PARENTS

The 5 Love Languages of Children
GARY CHAPMAN, PhD
ROSS CAMPBELL, MD

The 5 Love Languages of Teenagers
GARY CHAPMAN

Gary Chapman & Ross Campbell, M.D.
how to really LOVE your ADULT child

## FAMILIES

GARY CHAPMAN
The Family You've Always Wanted

101 conversation starters for families
GARY CHAPMAN & RAMON PRESSON

A Perfect Pet for Peyton
GARY CHAPMAN

FOR MORE INFORMATION VISIT 5LOVELANGUAGES.COM/RESOURCES/BOOKS

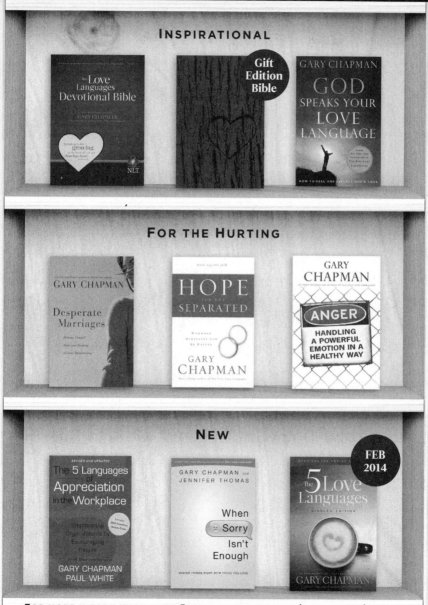

# GIFTABLE RESOURCES

## INSPIRATIONAL

## FOR THE HURTING

## NEW

FOR MORE INFORMATION VISIT 5LOVELANGUAGES.COM/RESOURCES/BOOKS